FACT
FINDER

HORSES
AND PONIES

FACT
FINDER

HORSES
AND PONIES

L E S L E Y · E C C L E S

CRESCENT BOOKS
New York

A SALAMANDER BOOK

First published by Salamander Books Ltd., 129/137 York Way,
London N7 9LG, United Kingdom.

©Salamander Books Ltd 1989

This 1989 edition published by Crescent Books, distributed by Crown
Publishers, Inc., 225 Park Avenue South, New York, New York 10003.

Printed and bound in Belgium.

ISBN 0-517-69206-6

h g f e d c b a

CREDITS

Editor: Jilly Glassborow
American Consultant: Leslie Ward
Designer: Liz Black
Artwork: John Francis
Filmset: The Old Mill, London
Color separation: Scantrans Pte Ltd., Singapore

Printed in Belgium by Proost International Book Production

PICTURE CREDITS

The publishers would like to thank the following photographers
and agencies for supplying the photographs for this book.
Photographs have been credited on the page: (B) Bottom,
(T) Top, (BR) Bottom right and (BL) Bottom left.

Sonia Halliday: 12(BR)
Kit Houghton: 9, 27, 33(B), 39, 40, 43, 45, 46, 47, 49, 50, 51, 55(B),
59, 61, 62, 63
Hulton Picture Library: 13(B)
Bob Langrish: Front cover, Back cover, 1, 3, 6, 8, 10, 11, 13(T), 14, 15, 16, 17,
18, 19, 20, 21, 22, 23, 24, 25, 26, 28, 29, 30, 31, 32, 33(T), 34, 53, 55(T), 57
Mansell Collection: 12(T)
Ronald Sheridan: 12(BL)

CONTENTS

PART ONE

INTRODUCTION TO HORSES AND PONIES

Challenging, exciting and powerful, horses and ponies have played a major part throughout Man's history, not only in war, agriculture and industry but, more importantly today, in a wide range of leisure pursuits. Illustrated in full colour throughout, this easy-to-use guide covers every aspect of horsemanship from the everyday basics of horse care and riding technique to more spectacular events such as show jumping, racing and trekking holidays. There are chapters on the horse's evolution, behaviour and methods of communication as well as information on the horse's working role and the numerous sporting events in which horses participate. The second part of the book covers over 35 of the most popular breeds across the world and introduces you to some fascinating facts about each breed's history and development.

Left: A pony and rider enjoying themselves in a one-day event. Their partnership is emphasized by a bold confident attitude over the fence, with both pony and rider looking eagerly forwards.

EVOLUTION OF THE HORSE

If the ancestors of the modern horse were suddenly to appear on earth today, they would not be easily recognizable as relatives of the horses and ponies we all know. It has taken over fifty five million years for the horse to reach its present state of development. By comparison, the evolution of Man took something like one five-hundredth of this time.

The first of the horse's ancestors, called *Eohippus*, was about the size of a fox and would have weighed around 5kg (12lb). He had four toes on his forefeet and three toes behind, all with very thick, strong, horny nails. As he would have lived in forests, it is likely that his coat would have had a dark background with spots or blotches on it for camouflage purposes.

Eohippus was a browsing animal, eating soft leaves from low-growing shrubs, rather than grazing like our modern horses. His teeth were therefore different, being more like a monkey's than a horse's. Instead of fleeing from his enemies, *Eohippus* hid from predators. His eyes were at the front of his head, unlike later horses who needed virtually all-round vision.

Between 40 and 25 million years ago *Mesohippus* and *Merychippus* came on to the scene. They differed from *Eohippus* in that they were larger, had a more advanced tooth structure and were three-toed animals. *Merychippus* succeeded *Mesohippus* and stood around 1m (39in) high. One development was that *Merychippus*, although three-toed, put more weight on to the central toe than did his ancestor.

It was changes in the Miocene epoch (a period in the Earth's history that lasted from 26 to 7 million years ago) that led to significant steps forward in the development of the horse. Browsing animals had been well suited to the forests and jungles but, as the climate changed, becoming drier, so the environment changed to treeless plains and steppe lands. To survive, animals had to adapt (become adjusted) to the new environment.

During the Miocene epoch gradual changes took place to the horse's ancestor: the neck became longer so the animal could graze more easily; the legs became longer for ease of grazing and for flight from enemies; the teeth became stronger and were used in a grinding action whilst the muzzle became longer to accommodate the flat molar teeth;

Above: *Connemara ponies are tough and hardy, able to withstand severe weather and sparse grazing. In order to survive, ponies had to adapt to their harsh environment.*

Below: *The horse's evolution. Along the base of the diagram time is shown in millions of years and geological epochs. The development of the horse's hoof is also shown.*

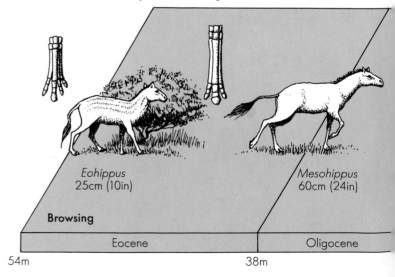

Eohippus
25cm (10in)

Mesohippus
60cm (24in)

Browsing

| Eocene | Oligocene |

54m   38m

8

and the eyes changed to a position nearer the sides of the head. Now that it lived in open grassland, the horse's ancestor needed to be fully aware of oncoming danger.

About six million years ago came the first animal to more closely resemble the modern horse of today. *Pliohippus* was the first single-toed horse and at the head he stood about 1.25m (50in) high.

If we could step back in time about a million years we would meet *Equus*. By this time our horse's ancestor stood around 1.3m (52in) high and was single-toed. On the underside of the hoof was a rubbery mass known as the 'frog', vital for absorbing shocks, for grip and for the circulation of blood in the foot.

Although *Equus* appears to have originated in North America, primitive horses spread to many continents across the land bridge which once joined North America to Asia. In Europe, Asia and Africa, various types of *Equus* developed according to local conditions and vegetation. For instance, small hardy ponies coped best in the mountainous regions whereas areas with good rainfall and plentiful supplies of food produced heavier types of horses.

The Modern Horse

There are a great many different breeds today and a number of theories on the origins of our modern horse. One theory points to four different types, all of which were domesticated. Basically these are: a pony

Above: *The oldest pure-bred horse in the world, the Arab has had great influence on other breeds. This stallion's alert ears and flaring nostrils indicate that something in the distance has attracted his attention.*

found in North Western Europe which would have been similar to the English Exmoor pony; a heavier-built pony native to northern Eurasia, with a dun (yellowish) coat, eel-stripe and a coarser head, like Przewalski's horse; a horse from the central Asian areas with a long narrow head and shallow hooves, standing about 15 hands; and finally, a small, fine-boned animal from Western Asia measuring about 12 hands. Today, horses are commonly measured in hands: a hand equals four inches (10cm).

No-one really knows when the horse was first domesticated by Man. Although it was relatively easy for Man to domesticate dogs, cattle and goats, the horse's size and the difficulty of capturing it and keeping it meant that the horse was left alone. However, it is generally thought that nomadic steppe people in Eurasia were the first to domesticate the horse, about 5-6,000 years ago.

Man has always hunted the horse — early cave drawings are evidence of this — but with domestication the horse became a source of transport, clothing, shelter and milk. Horses were ridden, driven and used as pack animals.

So began Man's association with the horse, a partnership which was greatly to affect the progress of Man and civilisation. Horses have played invaluable roles in the progress of agriculture, transport, the economy and industry, and, indeed, in the rise and fall of empires. It can be said that Man's history really has been carried on the back of the horse!

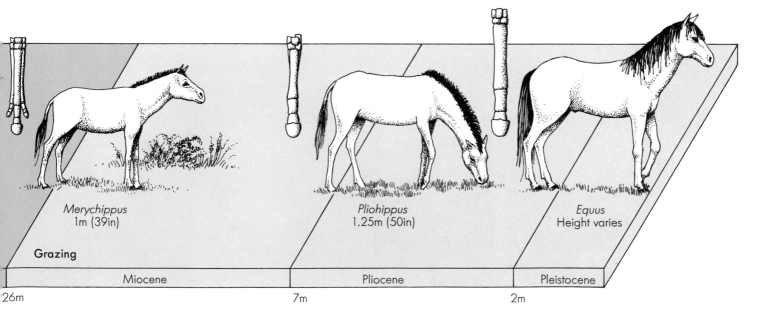

Merychippus
1m (39in)

Pliohippus
1.25m (50in)

Equus
Height varies

Grazing

Miocene	Pliocene	Pleistocene

26m   7m   2m

In the human world we have numerous languages and dialects with the result that if, for instance, a Russian person wishes to communicate with an English person then he will have to learn English or vice versa. Yet in the horse world the animals have a universal means of communication. A horse can express himself and be understood by other horses in several ways: through calls such as neighs, whinnies, squeals and snorts; by his body posture; or by the use of his ears, tail, neck, legs, mouth and head.

By watching horses at work and play it is possible to understand their system of communication — all of which adds up to a greater appreciation of our equine partners which, in turn, makes riding and handling horses even more enjoyable.

In the wild, horses live in herds and within this social structure have their own friends. Usually you can spot the friends as they will stick together when the herd moves, will graze close by each other and will indulge in mutual grooming. This behaviour is reflected in our domesticated horses — horses are very gregarious animals and often fret if deprived of company. They prefer their

Above: *Foals spend most of their days in play. This has a purpose, teaching them how to behave, and how to express themselves and understand the signals of other horses.*

Below: *A wild horse tries to get rid of any predators on its back by bucking. The rodeo horse reacts similarly to a rider.*

own kind but owners who have just one horse kept at home often keep goats or sheep to ensure the horse has companions.

If you watch a group of horses out at grass, after a while you can identify who is friends with whom. If two horses are friends, usually one is more dominant. And if another horse tries to intrude on the friendship it is quite likely that he will be seen off — the horse doing the 'clearing off' will display signs such as laid back ears and head shaking towards the intruder, and will threaten to bite.

Horses can recognize each other by the sounds of their neighs — and this call can mean a variety of things, from "where are you?" to "hello". The shorter, lower sounds known as nickers are used amongst friends — and of course horses often greet their human friends with nickers, particularly when it is feeding time!

In the wild a horse would warn his companions of danger by snorting. Most horse owners will have experienced their horse snorting when confronted with, for instance, a piece of farm machinery which is unexpectedly blocking a bridleway. Usually this snorting is accompanied by a change in the horse's body posture — his head is raised, he is more on his toes and moves with jerky steps. All this indicates that something alarming is happening — signals that can be read by other horses and by humans 'in the know' about the horse's language.

People and Horses

Just as we can read a horse's body language so he can read ours. If you are tense and frightened in the presence of a horse he will sense this and be alarmed. In circumstances where a horse is startled, afraid or faced with something he cannot understand then his natural reaction is to run away.

For example, a young horse placed in a field close to traffic for the first time will inevitably gallop off when a huge lorry thunders past. Yet by careful, firm, kind training, the horse can be taught to accept traffic. However, his human trainer must understand fully how and why a horse reacts as it does and be able to deal sympathetically with a horse's behaviour.

Many newcomers to horses do not know how to handle them and wonder why the horse bites or kicks out at them. Although a horse has virtually all-round vision he cannot see directly behind him and is likely to be startled if someone walks up from the rear — for instance, he may lash out. All that is needed is for the person to speak so that the horse is aware that someone is there.

Watch a horse's ears — for they tell you a great deal about the horse's concentration. For instance, if he is dozing they will be half-back; if he has spotted something interesting across the field they will be pricked and pointed forwards; if they are laid flat back against his head then do not approach the horse. His ears are indicating anger and fear, so it would be wise to restrain yourself from trying to pat the horse.

The behaviour of young foals is very interesting to observe. Just as a puppy shows his submission to bigger dogs by rolling on to his back, so foals have special submission signals. They 'mouth' at anything larger than themselves, whether it be horses, humans or other objects. The foal's teeth are exposed, his ears are drooped and his neck is stretched forward. When they are yearlings, the youngsters tend to stop mouthing but the more timid young horses may continue to

use their submission signals until they are are as much as two years old.

Most people will have seen horses pawing at the ground — this can be a sign of frustration, such as occurs when a stallion can see his mares but can gain no access to them. Horses also paw the ground in winter to remove snow from the grass and to break ice on water.

Horses are not naturally aggressive animals — in the past they hid or ran from enemies. They will only fight if absolutely necessary and, instead, try to sort out their differences by threatening. Take for instance the horse which likes to eat its food in peace and quiet. If disturbed by a human who insists on trying to groom him whilst he is feeding then the horse may deal with the problem by swinging his rump round and perhaps lifting a hindleg, so indicating that he may kick.

The behaviour of horses and the way in which they communicate is a fascinating subject — if you want to learn more there are a number of books available which will help you to understand and interpret what you have observed by 'horse-watching'.

Below: *If a young foal strays from its mother, the mother will call it back. Often a foal cannot recognize its mother, so it is up to mares to turn away foals other than their own.*

Right: *Horses can communicate their feelings with various movements of the head and body. In order to better understand a horse, it is a good thing to recognize the signs.*

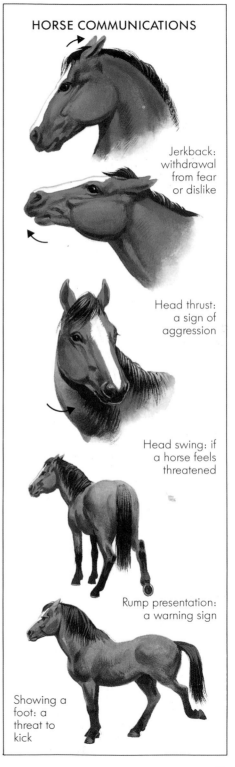

HORSE COMMUNICATIONS

Jerkback: withdrawal from fear or dislike

Head thrust: a sign of aggression

Head swing: if a horse feels threatened

Rump presentation: a warning sign

Showing a foot: a threat to kick

FAMOUS HORSES

As the horse has played such an important part in the history of Man it is not surprising that through the ages some horses have become famous in their own right.

Some of the best known horses are mythological, such as Pegasus, the winged horse who wears a golden bridle and is the offspring of Poseidon and Medusa in Greek mythology. Another of the legendary winged horses is Al Borak, Mohammed's horse who was white with a human head.

Of the real life horses, one of the most famous of ancient times was that belonging to Alexander the Great. Bucephalus was given to Alexander when the future king was a young boy, and no-one except Alexander could break or ride him. The horse carried his master on many campaigns, dying in India in 326 BC.

The Roman Emperor Caligula was so obsessed with his horse Incitatus, that the animal was made a citizen of Rome, then appointed as senator and would have had the ultimate honour of a consulship bestowed upon him but for the assassination of Caligula in AD 41.

Below: Like many ancient peoples, the Ancient Greeks admired the horse's grace and power, here symbolized in the mythical winged horse Pegasus.

Incitatus had originally been known as Porcellus, meaning 'little pig', but when he started to win races he was renamed. Thereafter Caligula kept his horse in a marble stable. The manger was made from ivory and the bucket from gold.

The Horses of Napoleon and Wellington

Napoleon Bonaparte, Emperor of France, owned over a hundred horses of various breeds but he had a particular liking for grey Arabs. During campaigns in Egypt and Syria he captured many Arab horses and brought them to France to found national stud farms.

His favourite mount was a 14.1 hand grey Arab stallion named Marengo. Foaled in Egypt, the horse came to France as a six-year-old. His new master first rode him at the Battle of Marengo in 1800 and Napoleon was so delighted with the little horse's courage that he named the stallion after his victory.

It was to be fifteen years before Napoleon fought his last battle at Waterloo, but Marengo went on all of Napoleon's campaigns in between. On eight occasions the stallion was wounded.

Marengo was captured by the victorious British at Waterloo and was taken to England where he was sent to stud. He died when he was 38 and his skeleton can be seen at the National Army Museum in London.

Above: Napoleon was often depicted riding grey Arabs, of which he was particularly fond. His most famous Arab mount was Marengo.

Below: Alexander the Great astride his favourite mount, Bucephalus. Alexander's stature as world conqueror was enhanced by his mastery of this hitherto untameable steed.

Napoleon's British adversary at Waterloo was the Duke of Wellington whose favourite horse, Copenhagen, was noted for his endurance and courage.

A 15.1 hand chestnut stallion, Copenhagen was famous well before he became the mount of Wellington. His grandsire was the famous Eclipse and his dam took part in the siege of Copenhagen — which is why her offspring was given his name.

Copenhagen trained as a racehorse before being sold as a charger and taken to Spain where the British were fighting the French. Here he was spotted by the Duke of Wellington and, although Copenhagen was spirited, with a reputation of being difficult to handle, the Iron Duke and his new horse seemed to 'gel' together.

Together Copenhagen and the Duke fought many battles but their most testing and the last was Waterloo. The day before the battle the Duke had ridden Copenhagen nearly 100 km (60 miles)!

Following the famous victory of Waterloo the valiant stallion went to the Duke's Hampshire home to spend his days in peace and quiet. He died in 1836 and was buried with full military honours.

Famous Horses of the 20th Century

Two Argentine Criollo horses gained great fame when they travelled 16,000 km (10,000 miles) from Buenos Aires to Washington in the USA. Mancha, aged 16, and Gato, aged 15, were accompanied by Felix Tschiffely, who undertook his momentous ride to prove the stamina of the Criollo breed, which he believed to be dying out. The journey began on St George's Day in 1925 and took two and a half years, with man and horses enduring many hardships, including extremes of heat and cold. Gato died at the age of 36 and Mancha died aged 40.

One of the most famous and influential American racehorses was Man o' War who was born in 1917. He was known as Big Red because of his impressive build and fiery chestnut colour. In 21 races he was beaten only once and the jockey's incompetence was blamed for that defeat. He broke seven records in his three-year-old season. Other great racehorses such as Sir Ivor and Never Say Die trace back to Man o' War.

Another famous and highly popular horse of the turf was the champion British steeplechaser Arkle who was owned by the Duchess of Westminster. Foaled in 1957, Arkle won 27 out of 35 races but retired in 1966 after fracturing a bone in his foot. The

Above: Red Rum's courage, character and intelligence endeared him to racegoers. His remarkable Grand National career (three firsts, and two seconds) is unmatched.

Below: The superb Man o' War, a sire of proven quality whose descendants are still winning races today, was beaten only once in a three-year racing career.

fracture happened during the King George VI steeplechase at Kempton Park in England and Arkle continued running, finishing second. A life-size statue of him stands at Cheltenham racecourse.

Perhaps the most famous horse of modern times is Red Rum, the racehorse who had all the odds stacked against him but who went on to become a fairytale legend and a national hero.

Born in Ireland in 1965, he was from a line of sprinters — but his mother was branded crazy and unraceable. As a yearling Red Rum was sold to England. His first victory in a flat race was at Aintree, later to be the scene of his heroic conquests.

Then fate struck its blow — for 'Rummy' was diagnosed as having a potentially crippling bone disease. The gelding was sold and his new owner took him home to a tiny racing yard tucked away behind a garage in the side streets of Southport.

Eight months later, in 1973, Red Rum galloped to his first Grand National win, smashing the course record which had stood for 39 years! His initial victory was followed by triumphs the following year and in 1977. In between Red Rum notched up two runner-up placings. Sadly, a bruised heel ended his racing days just before the 1978 National.

Riding stands apart from other sports because, to be a successful rider, you are relying on more than your own abilities.

Athletes, tennis players and footballers have only themselves to think about in preparing for any competition but riders have to ensure that their horses are fit and properly prepared as well as themselves. It is the challenge of achieving harmony and understanding with a live animal which keeps many people hooked on riding.

Of course, riding has many other attractions. It's a way of relaxing after a hectic day's work, and travelling by horse-back is one of the best ways to see and enjoy the countryside. Riding is also a mental and physical challenge which you can enjoy at many different levels — tens of thousands of people ride simply for pleasure and have no wish to extend their riding further. Yet for those with a competitive streak there are shows and events throughout the year covering all aspects of riding horses.

To learn to ride it is best to have lessons from a qualified instructor at an approved or recognized riding school. You will probably find that initial lessons will be 'on the

THE CORRECT RIDING POSITION

A good riding position: ideally ear, shoulder, hip and heel are in line.

Sit centrally in the saddle with your weight equally distributed on each side.

Left: *Working on the lunge is excellent for riders at all levels. It increases your balance and feel for the horse's movement.*

lunge'. This is where the instructor has control of the horse via a 'lunge rein' and works the horse in a large circle. The rider therefore has the opportunity to become accustomed to the movement and feel of the horse without having to worry about steering.

The Riding Position
Riders should adopt a certain 'position' on the horse to make it easier both for the horse to carry their weight and for them to give the horse instructions.

Basically, a rider should sit in the deepest part of the saddle, with his or her weight evenly distributed — neither collapsing to one side nor leaning backwards or forwards. The upper body should be upright but without any tension, the rider looking ahead, arms close in to the sides with the elbows bent.

When viewed from the side there ought to be a straight line from the horse's bit, through the reins, the rider's hands and lower arms to the rider's elbows. You should also be able to draw a straight line through the rider's ear, shoulder, hip and heel (see the illustration opposite).

Riders should keep their legs in light contact with the horse's sides, maintaining a slight bend in the knees and taking their weight down through the heels. The feet should be placed in the stirrups so that the balls of the feet rest on the stirrup irons. In the correct position the toes should be pointing forwards.

Riding Aids

A horse is trained to react to certain signals from its rider. These signals are called aids and take two forms — natural and artificial. Natural aids are the rider's seat and weight, legs, hands, voice and power of thought. Artificial aids include whips and spurs.

Horses are very sensitive animals and will sense any nervousness or fear on the part of their rider. For instance, if a rider is afraid of tackling a jump, perhaps because of previous bad experiences, then the rider's apprehension will transmit to the horse who may well refuse to jump or may jump awkwardly because of lack of positive instructions from the person on its back.

The Gaits of the Horse

Horses have three different paces or gaits and the rider has to adapt to the different speeds and requirements of each pace.

Walking is said to be a four-time gait, with the horse picking up and putting down each leg in a certain order — left hind leg, followed by left foreleg, then right hind leg followed by right foreleg. Riders can soon learn to feel the sequence of the movement. To ask the horse to walk on, the rider closes his or her legs around the horse's sides and eases the pressure or contact on the reins.

It is important to realize that a horse's head and neck act as a balancing pole. Riders therefore need sympathetic hands which follow the movement of the horse's head so that they do not upset the horse's balance or jar him in the mouth.

The trot is the next pace up from walk and the horse moves in a different way. Trot is a two-time gait because the horse moves his legs in diagonal pairs — the off-fore and near-hind legs together and the near-fore and off-hind legs together.

Riders can either sit or rise to the trot. Sitting trot can be quite bumpy at first until the rider has learnt to relax and absorb the movement. Rising trot is more comfortable once

Above: *Riding outside the familiar confines of the school's arena calls for extra alertness. When travelling along public highways, be sure to keep your mind on your riding and be aware of other road users.*

the rider has mastered the art of letting the horse's stride help him or her to leave the saddle. This comes with practice.

In the rising trot, as the horse trots in a one-two, one-two movement, the rider should accompany the horse with a rhythmic rise-sit, rise-sit movement.

The canter, the third of the horse's gaits, is a progression from trot and is very comfortable. It is a three-time gait in which one diagonal pair of legs moves together and the legs of the other pair move independently.

If a cantering horse is asked to go faster he will gallop but at this increased speed the way in which he moves his legs changes again, this time to a four-time sequence. During the gallop, a horse extends its head and neck and its stride reaches its maximum length.

Jumping

Once you have mastered the art of walking, trotting and cantering, and have a reasonably secure, independent seat, you may progress to jumping.

When riding, it is essential that the rider stays in balance with the horse — and when it comes to jumping this means that the rider needs to alter position. As a horse jumps his centre of gravity moves forward because his

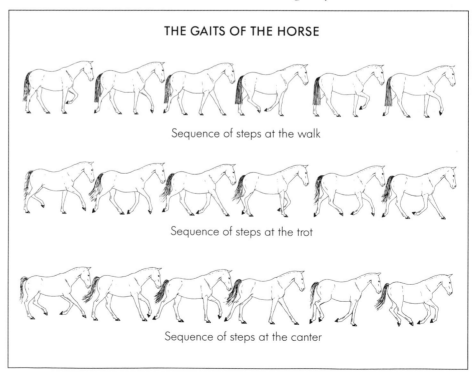

THE GAITS OF THE HORSE

Sequence of steps at the walk

Sequence of steps at the trot

Sequence of steps at the canter

head and neck are stretched out so the rider also has to shift his or her balance forward.

When a horse jumps he lengthens and elevates his stride. For smaller jumps, such as 60cm (2ft), there is more lengthening of the stride than elevation, but over a 1.4m (4ft 6in) fence, there will be considerable elevation too. The degree to which the rider shifts weight forward to stay in balance with the horse will vary according to the size and type of fence being tackled.

In jumping position the rider folds from the hips, maintains the usual leg position, follows the movements of the horse's head with the hands, keeps a straight back and looks ahead. The seat remains in light contact with the saddle although over larger jumps the rider will be just out of the saddle.

To help you achieve this position your stirrups should be shortened by at least two holes. This closes the angles at your knees, ankles and hips so making it easier for you to maintain your balance.

Most riders are introduced to jumping by negotiating poles on the ground at first, then building up to small jumps after the poles. The jumps will probably be cross-poles as

Above: *Top show jumper Paul Schockemohle and Next Deister. Notice the arc of the horse's body and how the rider shifts position in line with the horse's centre of gravity.*

the shape helps to guide the horse and rider to the centre of the fence.

A good way of building riders' confidence over jumps is to send them through some grids which consist of a series of small fences and poles set in a line. This gridwork also helps a horse and rider to become more athletic, sharpening their reactions and increasing their suppleness.

Variety can be added to lessons by tackling small cross country fences as well as show jumps. Whereas show jumps will fall down if knocked, cross-country fences are more solid and make use of natural features such as hedges and ditches.

Riding courses
The natural progression from jumping single fences and grids is to tackle a course of jumps. A typical show jumping course may include ten fences and several changes of direction — quite a task at first!

Below: *Jumping small natural obstacles such as logs is a good way of introducing novice riders to the basics of jumping technique, and builds confidence.*

16

RIDING TIPS

• Mount from the nearside, but be able to mount from the offside as well.

• Keep firm but gentle contact through the reins with your horse's mouth — imagine you are holding a live bird in your hands.

• Check your stirrups are the correct length by measuring them alongside your arm. With your fingertips against the stirrup bar, the bottom of the stirrup iron should reach your armpit.

Walk the course on foot before you ride it so that you can get the order of fences firmly in your mind and make mental notes of where the fences are sited. Fences along the edges of the arena are easier to ride than those in the middle as the ring side helps to keep you straight. When you begin, approach each fence centrally. You may have to go around other fences to position yourself for a jump — make use of the whole arena, not forgetting the corners.

The course may include a combination fence, consisting of two or three jumps. Do not just ride the first element, but keep your eyes fixed beyond the final part and ride the complete sequence of jumps.

Establish a good working canter before you set off for the first jump of a course. At first you may find it easier to cope with changes of direction by coming down to a trot from canter. But strike off into canter again in plenty of time for the next fence. Think of riding a balanced, flowing round and have the course in your mind as a whole, not as separate entities. Just concentrate on maintaining a strong, active canter and be prepared to go with your horse's movement.

Riding for the Disabled

For many disabled people, the opportunity to ride a horse or pony opens new horizons. Being on horseback may represent the only time they are able to move around without relying on someone else. Riding has also helped many disabled people with their co-ordination, mobility, and balance.

Organizations involved in this work include the North American Riding for the Handicapped Association and the British Riding for the Disabled Association. Local groups give mentally and physically handicapped people immeasurable pleasure. The ponies and horses used for this work are stars in their own right. They need to be strong, kind and totally reliable. As horses are very sensitive animals they seem to appreciate that they must take special care of their disabled riders.

Below: *Working through grids of fences and/or poles helps riders to become more positive and to use their legs to better effect.*

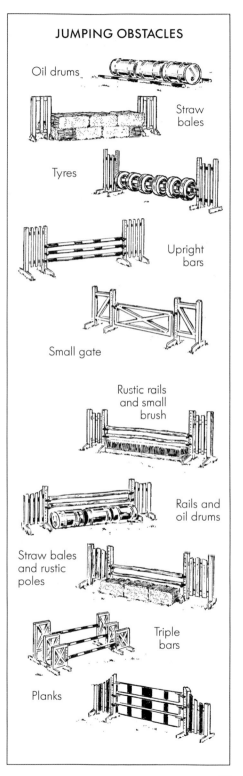

JUMPING OBSTACLES

Oil drums

Straw bales

Tyres

Upright bars

Small gate

Rustic rails and small brush

Rails and oil drums

Straw bales and rustic poles

Triple bars

Planks

Once they have mastered the basic skills, many people find that they reach a plateau in their riding. They seem to make little progress and the weekly riding lesson can become rather repetitive. One of the best ways of overcoming this feeling is to go on a riding holiday. A concentrated week of riding new horses, in different surroundings and meeting new challenges, is guaranteed to revitalize your interest and boost your riding skills.

Many types of riding holidays are available all over the world — you can trek across Iceland; try out a dude ranch in the USA; ride the Pennine Way, the backbone of England; or sample hunting in Ireland, the Mecca for 'horsey' people and particularly those interested in hunting.

Holiday companies are becoming more adept at the equestrian holiday business and offer various packages. Apart from specialist holidays it is usually possible to find riding available in or near some of the more popular tourist resorts across the world.

Equestrian holidays may be based around leisure riding, such as hacking over beautiful countryside, or they may be instruction based. These latter holidays can either be general riding weeks or based around one discipline such as dressage or long distance riding. Alternatively, you could possibly try a new equestrian sport — for instance polo, driving or Western riding. It is also possible in some countries to work towards riding and stable management examinations as part of your holiday.

Whatever your inclination, someone will have a holiday suited to you. In addition, many centres operate very flexibly to cater for their guests' individual requirements.

The Necessary Level of Experience
For general riding holidays you ought to be competent at walk, trot and canter, be safe enough to get over small jumps and be able to keep full control of your horse when riding in a group.

There is little point in over-stating your riding skills when considering a riding holi-

Right: *What better way to appreciate the natural beauty of a country than by seeing it from horseback? These riders are enjoying the desert scenery around Phoenix, Arizona, in the United States.*

day. If you are not capable of riding fit hunters across the Irish countryside then a hunting holiday will certainly not enrich your riding experience.

Many relatively new riders fail to realize the difference between riding in indoor schools and tackling the wide open spaces. However, if you are sensible in your choice of holiday, stretching your abilities a little, but not so much that you frighten yourself, you should find that a riding holiday will give you more confidence and your balance, co-ordination and general riding ability will have improved.

Making the Most of your Holiday
A little preparation beforehand can make a great deal of difference to your holiday. When choosing a holiday look carefully at the centre's brochures for an idea of the type of horses you will be riding, the local countryside and the accommodation you will be living in for a while.

If you are holidaying in your own country and it is at all possible, it is worth visiting the centre before committing yourself. There are many good centres but unfortunately there are also some less than reputable ones where standards of safety and horse care leave something to be desired.

Chat to the owners over the telephone, asking them to explain what a week's riding

Above: *Relaxing on a beach, with a difference. The carefree Caribbean way of life is reflected in the riding style of these Jamaican holiday-makers.*

usually entails, in terms of hours in the saddle, terrain traversed, how much you are expected to do in respect of your mount's care, and what safety measures they adopt.

Many centres will provide testimonials from previous holidaymakers. If so, try to contact one of these for a first hand account of the holiday.

Having decided where you are going, do make sure you are fit. Five or six hours in the saddle can be extremely taxing so have a 'get fit' campaign prior to your holiday.

You should go prepared for all kinds of weather conditions, unless you are holidaying in an area where good weather is guaranteed. Remember to pack items such as fly repellent and a small first aid kit.

Your riding clothes should be your normal, comfortable gear. A cross country trail ride is not the time to break in new boots. Loose fitting shirts and jodhpurs are much more comfortable than restrictive clothing such as tight jeans.

If you have little experience of riding on roads, or across mountains, rivers and so on, try to familiarize yourself with the correct procedures before you go. Knowing about road etiquette and how you should ride up steep slopes will take some of the apprehension out of these events when they actually happen!

RIDING ON A SLOPE

Going downhill: sit tall, keep your horse straight and let him balance himself.

Riding uphill: lean forwards and steady yourself by holding on to the mane.

Keeping your own horse is more than just a hobby, pastime or sport — it is a way of life. Horses are totally reliant on their owners for food, water, exercise, shelter and their good health, and accordingly demand a great deal of time and money.

There are various ways of keeping horses. If you have adequate land and stabling facilities you can keep them on your own premises. Alternatively, you can rent grazing and stabling, or you can place the horse in livery, that is, in the total care of someone else whose business it is to provide the facilities and time that some owners cannot provide themselves. This latter method works very well for riders who have demanding full-time jobs but who still wish to have the pleasure of their own horse.

Some horses and ponies can be kept out at grass all year round, for example, the native ponies of Britain are hardy and used to being out in all kinds of weather conditions. Certain breeds, on the other hand, such as Thoroughbreds, would not fare well if left out in extremely bad weather. All types of horses and ponies, however, benefit from a daily period out at grass in order to relax and enjoy themselves. It would be totally unfair

to keep an equine shut up in a stable 24 hours a day, with the only relief being perhaps an hour's exercise.

Horses that are left stabled for long periods become bored and this can lead to the formation of bad habits such as weaving (when the horse sways from side to side constantly) which can damage the horse physically as well as mentally.

Exercise

Exercise is another important item on the daily agenda for the horse owner. Unless the horse is off work through illness or a well-deserved holiday, then he needs to be worked regularly to keep fit.

Again, if the horse's basic requirement is not met, problems can occur. These may manifest themselves in health difficulties or behavioural problems in the stable or when ridden. Prevention is better than cure.

The amount of work a horse receives will depend on his age, level of fitness, what competitions or events are in store for him in the near future, the time available to the owner (although if this is always limited then alternative arrangements must be made to ensure the horse is properly exercised) and the type

Above: *Horses enjoy a variety of feeds — including hay, barley, oats, bran, maize, nuts, chaff, coarse mix and sugar beet. It is essential to provide a well balanced diet for a horse to meet the animal's individual needs, according to its age, work load and so on.*

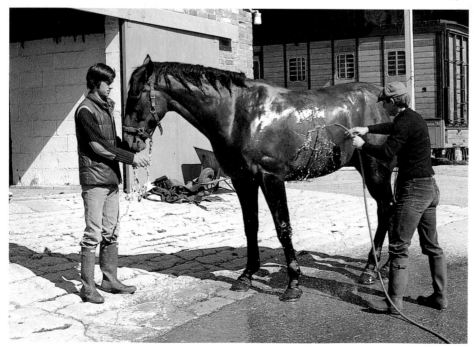

FACT FILE

- Horses should not be worked for an interval of 60-90 minutes after completing their feed.

- For good digestion, horses need lots of bulk food such as hay and grass.

- The normal temperature of a horse is 37.7-38°C (100-100.5°F). If it rises more than two degrees, call the vet immediately.

- At rest a horse will take from 8-15 breaths a minute and his pulse will be 36-42 beats a minute.

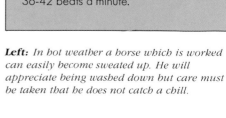

Left: *In hot weather a horse which is worked can easily become sweated up. He will appreciate being washed down but care must be taken that he does not catch a chill.*

of exercise planned — two hours hacking gently around the lanes is totally different from 40 minutes hard schooling over jumps.

Feeding

Horses eat little and often, so owners must consider this when working out a feeding routine. Whereas dogs can survive on one big meal a day, a horse cannot — his stomach is designed to be always two-thirds full and long periods without food will cause stress and digestive problems. Water is another essential — horses drink 20-40 litres (6-10 gals) a day so they must always have a clean, fresh supply available.

There is an art to feeding horses, and it is vital that each horse is treated as an individual and its diet fine-tuned to its needs. Wavering from this path may result in poorly animals or behavioural problems.

Having provided the basic daily needs of food, water, shelter and exercise, a horse owner's responsibility does not finish.

Grooming

Grooming your horse — attending to his feet and coat — should also be part of the horse owner's daily programme. There are more benefits to this than simply improving the appearance of the horse. Daily grooming stimulates the horse's circulation, improves his muscle tone and helps to prevent disease by keeping the animal clean.

It is also a useful way of ensuring that the horse is checked over daily for any cuts, injuries or warning signs (such as heat in the legs) of problems to come.

Shoeing and Veterinary Care

Horses need regular attention from a qualified farrier — most animals need re-shoeing every four to six weeks. Costs are also incurred through routine as well as unexpected visits from the veterinary surgeon. Innoculations and tooth inspections are just two of the annual 'musts'. In addition there may be call-outs if the horse injures himself, such as straining a tendon whilst competing.

It is vital that horses are wormed regularly to combat the potential damage of ascarids and strongyles. Worm infestation is debilitating and can even result in death.

Caring for the Equipment

Of course, there is more than just the horse to look after. The amount of equipment horse owners gather around themselves is phenomenal. The basics alone are: stable tools such as a pitchfork, shovel, brush and skip; feed storage bins; a grooming kit; water and feed buckets; haynets; a first aid kit; saddlery, including saddle, girth, stirrup irons and leathers, bridle and bit; a head-collar and leading rope; rugs; protective boots for schooling and travelling; and tack cleaning materials.

All this equipment needs to be kept clean and in good condition — for the safety of horse and rider as well as ensuring that your investment in the gear is returned by prolonged service.

Below: *Owning your own horse means investing in a vast amount of equipment. Even if you do not compete there are still many items which a horse needs, such as saddlery, rugs and grooming kits. A selection of the most common items is shown here.*

As soon as the horse had been domesticated he started to be used to enlarge Man's power and influence. He became Man's ally in times of war and conquest, and his training was developed for the purposes of war. For instance, nomadic tribes domesticated the horse because hunting on horseback was more successful than hunting on foot. But they soon discovered that horses could also assist them in making war on their neighbours so that more land and grazing could be obtained.

For centuries the primary use of the horse was in war. Although horses were also used in peace time, for pulling heavy loads or as transport, they were not involved in 'work' to the same degree as other animals. Oxen, for example, were used for pulling carts in preference to horses as they were cheaper to keep and at the end of their working life could be fattened and sold for meat.

In some areas, such as Asia, the horse was held in such high esteem that the thought of using it for lowly tasks did not even cross peoples' minds. And in Europe, donkeys and mules were more suited than horses to working on the terrain, particularly on the narrow vineyard tracks.

Although horses were used for agricultural work in Europe in the 8th century, it was for only a limited amount of work. At that time the horses were not really big enough or strong enough, but by the 11th century bigger animals were being bred, even though they were for the purposes of war! These horses did play a part in the development of some of our current heavy horses such as the Shires and Ardennes.

Slowly, the horse started to have more involvement in agriculture, particularly as more sophisticated machinery was invented which was better suited to the quicker action of the horse than to the slow ox.

The early 1700s in Britain saw many agricultural implements being continually improved, as well as the appearance of innovations such as the horse-drawn seed drill. Horses were increasingly used in agriculture, having proved that they could work fast and efficiently; two horses pulling a new plough,

Left: *A revival of interest in heavier breeds has ensured the continuance of such magnificent sights as these plough horses, bedecked with traditional braiding.*

Above: *Some breweries have maintained tradition and keep Shires to pull drays, so promoting their company and helping the survival of the breed as well.*

Below: *Cavalry skills on the battlefield, such as agility, speed and accuracy, are demonstrated today by such peaceful activities as tent-pegging displays.*

the Arbuthnot, could work more land in a day than a team of six oxen.

Working the land required extremely strong horses and a number of heavy horse breeds developed all over the world. Perhaps the best known of all these is the Shire, developed in Britain.

All over Europe horses played a vital part in the progress of agriculture and in turn, the economies of their homelands, until the advent of motorized farm machinery ended the horse's dominance.

Transport and industry also depended upon horses. Horses were used for taking wagon loads of merchandise to ports; for providing the power to work wind and water mills; in the mines ponies were used to haul carts full of coal; barges for both freight and passengers were drawn along the canals using horses; there were even railway horses who hauled coaches over fairly short distances on tramways.

In the cities and rural areas horses were major forms of transport, pulling trams, coal carts, hearses, dust carts, cabs, delivering mail. The horse population was large and their working lives were harsh.

Today, in some countries of the world, horses still have primary roles in agriculture and transport. Unfortunately, in some areas, conditions for the horses have not improved a great deal since the harsh days of the 19th century and international equine charities are still working to improve the lot of the horse in certain countries.

Outside of agriculture and industry, working horses are to be found in many different spheres, such as in the police and army, in hunts and on ranches. In addition, horses are helping many disabled children and adults to lead more fulfilled lives.

Army Horses

For many centuries, horses have played an important part in our military history, so it is fitting that the horse is still very much a part of the modern armed forces.

This is particularly so in Britain where there is a tradition of horses being involved in the pomp and ceremony of state and royal occasions. For instance, the King's Troop Royal Horse Artillery has demonstrated its Musical Drive all over the world.

The Musical Drive involves recreating the atmosphere of battle: teams of six horses pull gun carriages with troops astride three of the horses in each team. Several manoeuvres are performed in the 20-minute performance. For instance, the gun teams stand at either end of the arena then, on command, they head for each other at full speed, passing in the centre of the arena and missing each other by a hair's breadth.

Another aspect of the display involves the gun team criss-crossing the arena at full gallop, demonstrating the precision timing and superb control required to avoid a crash.

Military displays such as this illustrate the supreme agility, obedience, ability, courage and skills of the horses, attributes which have

made the horse such a welcome partner of Man on the battlefield.

Many horses have lost their lives in war and even in peace time horses have not escaped from the horrors of terrorism. One army horse to capture the hearts and sympathy of the British public was Sefton, one of the Household Cavalry horses injured in the infamous IRA bombing at Hyde Park, London, in July 1982.

Several horses were killed and the 19 year-old Sefton, close to death, became the focus of the nation's attention as daily bulletins on the state of his health were issued. Happily, Sefton made a full recovery, becoming the star of the show at London's Horse of the Year Show later that year.

Police Horses

Whether on the streets of New York City or patrolling the quieter roads of an English town, police horses play an invaluable role, even in today's electronic world.

Horses are still one of the most effective means of crowd control. In addition, since people enjoy meeting and stroking the horses, they help maintain friendly relations between police and public.

Apart from the usual schooling given to any riding horse, police horses also learn to cope with heavy traffic and other distractions such as flag waving and jeering or even rioting crowds.

During their training, situations are carefully 'set up' so that the horses can learn and understand about all the various kinds of hazards they may meet before being faced with them in real life. For example, they are taught to negotiate tyres placed on the floor, and to walk across unstable flooring. And once the horses are ready to start working, older, more experienced, police horses accompany the new recruits to help increase their confidence.

Royal Canadian Mounted Police

The stirring and romantic sight of the Royal Canadian Mounted Police, in their striking red uniforms astride magnificent black horses, is well known all over the world.

The Mounties, as they are commonly called, were originally formed in 1873 to patrol the vast area of North America known as the North West Territories. At this time horses were the only means of transport across the plains. Nowadays, however, the Mounties patrol using cars, boats, planes and even snowmobiles. Their horses are used solely for parades, as escorts for visiting VIPs and

Above: Police horses are trained to move without hesitation past all kinds of hazards. Being amidst jostling, flag-waving crowds is one part of the job they learn to accept.

Below: The Royal Canadian Mounted Police perform their Musical Ride at venues all over the world, demonstrating the supreme skill of both horses and riders.

for displays. The displays include the internationally famous Musical Ride in which 32 riders and horses demonstrate movements used by cavalries during battles. This magnificent display requires precision timing and skill from both horse and rider.

All the horses in the force are black as this shows off the Mounties' uniforms. Close inspection of each horse's rump will reveal a stencil of a maple leaf, the national emblem of Canada.

Ontario is the home of the Police's own stud farm where the Mounties' horses are bred and trained. The horses are generally three-quarters to seven-eighths Thoroughbred and stand 15.3 to 17 hands.

Cattle Horses

Despite popular belief, horses which work cattle exist in countries other than the United States, where tales of cowboys and the Wild West are legendary.

Brazil, Canada, Australia and Argentina all have cattle horses. However, it is the USA which possesses one of the best breeds for this type of work: the agile, fast-moving Quarter Horse which has an in-built ability for working cattle — cutting out calves from

Above: Even today, horses are still the best way of performing some tasks on working ranches. For herding and cutting out cattle, the horse reigns supreme.

the herd and driving the cattle as a herd. The reputation of these horses is so high that many have been imported into Australia to work on the huge stations in the outback. Australia also has its own stock horse.

In Argentina the gauchos (cowboys) work cattle using the Criollo ponies. The best size for cattle horses is 14.2-16 hands. The horses need to be sure-footed, with the ability to stop, twist and turn easily. However, they must not be too excitable — equable temperaments are needed as working cattle requires patience and calmness.

Today's fast growing sport of Western riding requires horses and riders to demonstrate the manoeuvres a working cow horse would use. It is a totally different style of riding and horse training to the riding that many people learn.

Western riding reflects the philosophy of the early cowboys, that the horse cannot be dominated by the rider, but can work freely at the rider's request.

Although the horse was first domesticated so that he could be used for hunting, to act as a pack animal, and as transport, it was not long before he was used for another purpose. The horse gave pleasure to his masters, and, in addition to being a working animal, he was also used for recreation. Horses and riders raced against each other, and teams of players pitted their skills in polo.

Today, although some horses and ponies are still kept primarily to work, the vast majority of horses are now kept for recreational purposes. This may involve competing at the highest level in their sport with all its associated challenges and obstacles or simply being a family's cherished 'pet'.

A number of our modern sports, such as long distance riding, have developed out of the skills required in the normal working life of our horse's ancestors.

In all horse sports there is an added element which other sports people do not have to contend with. The rider has an animal partner to consider, and the horse's condition, training and relationship with his rider are all-important. The competitive horse person, as well as looking after his or her own fitness, also has to nurture a horse, bring him along in all the necessary skills, and ensure he is at peak fitness at the right time.

Equestrian sports are based on partnership, the special relationship between horse and rider. It is no easy task to produce a horse to top level competition: years of dedication and commitment are required.

A number of equestrian sports are outlined here — and it should be remembered that for all the riders who reach the top and become household names in their chosen disciplines, there are thousands more who

Above: *Television coverage of major competitions has helped show jumping to become one of the most popular equestrian sports. The top international riders and horses have become household names.*

are competing at a much lower level, putting in tremendous amounts of time and effort, and all because of one basic motivating force — they want to enjoy their horse and be part of him.

Show Jumping
Now one of the most popular equestrian sports in many different countries, show jumping has come a long way since its early days at the turn of this century. Today's show jumpers compete in front of large and enthusiastic audiences, whereas the first show jumping competition in France required the

competitors to parade in an arena and then jump fences outside. This was hardly exciting for any spectators!

The sport initially developed purely as 'leaping' competitions — in England horses entered for showing at the agricultural shows were also eligible for the jumping.

However, the sport was developing in other countries too and in 1912 was included in the Olympic Games for the first time. Nine years later a number of nations joined together in an attempt to standardize the rules for show jumping. This was the start of the FEI (Fédération Equestre Internationale) which is now the governing body of all international equestrian sport.

There is now a great variety of classes, such as the Puissance which is a test of jumping ability. Riders and horses tackle very large fences including a big wall. Other classes call for jumping ability and speed; world championships require riders to jump rounds on each other's horses so testing the riders' ability to get the best from each horse.

Show jumping classes provide colourful spectacles with their brightly painted fences and use of flowers, plants and shrubs around the obstacles. It is a sport requiring tremendous accuracy as well as gymnastic ability and speed from the horse. However, most countries have shows at all levels so that many riders can enjoy show jumping.

Dressage

The training of the riding horse in obedience and deportment is called dressage, a word derived from the French verb 'dresser' meaning 'to train'. In dressage, horses are trained to carry themselves in the best possible way and execute their natural paces in response to their rider's commands.

Of course, all riding horses undergo basic training or schooling to ensure they are obedient, supple and a pleasure to ride, and novice riders executing circles and serpentines (loops) as part of their riding lesson are all taking part in what is basically dressage.

Like all forms of training, dressage is progressive, with the basic steps being established before moving on to more difficult tasks. At the lower levels of dressage there are many riders competing, but as the training and commitment required becomes more intense so the numbers decrease. At its highest levels dressage presents a picture of a horse and rider in total harmony, exuding confidence, suppleness, and elegance.

If you watch a top rider in action you will notice that the rider's instructions to the horse are barely perceptible yet the animal is performing complicated movements with apparent ease. Behind this scene there lie many years of hard work striving to reach perfection, and a riding tradition which goes back many centuries.

When horses were used for battles it was essential that they were highly obedient and responsive. The Greek cavalry officer Xenophon, who wrote about the training of horses in 400 BC and has influenced riders and trainers ever since, taught that horses should respond to the lightest of aids and should show off their paces and abilities willingly. To achieve this there has to be a true understanding and partnership between horse and rider, all of which takes time.

During the Renaissance the first riding school was set up (in Naples, 1532) where horses were trained to perform intricate movements. However, there was little else established in this field until the Imperial Spanish Riding School opened in Vienna in 1735. Modern dressage training is based upon the principles of this world-famous school (see also Lipizzaners on page 54).

Competitive dressage involves riding a test — a set series of movements which is judged with marks awarded on a scale of 0 to 10. Marks are also awarded for the rider's position and seat, and the horse's paces, impulsion and submission.

Below: A Lipizzaner, Favory Wera, competing in Olympic dressage. Modern dressage training is founded on the principles of the Spanish Riding School in Vienna which is famous for its Lipizzaners.

Tests are ridden in an arena, either 20m by 40m (approximately 65ft by 130ft) at the lower levels or 20m by 60m (approximately 65ft by 195ft) for the more advanced tests. International tests include the movements required in Olympic tests (dressage has been an Olympic sport since 1912) with the ultimate being the Grand Prix test.

Tests performed to music have become popular. These are judged rather like skating, with marks awarded for technical merit and the interpretation of the music.

Eventing

Eventing is the supreme test of horse and rider, calling for ability, courage, fitness and versatility. The challenge of eventing has its origins in a military setting, for it was European cavalry officers who first devised a competition similar to that we now know as 'eventing' or 'horse trials'.

This sport involves three phases: a dressage test to demonstrate the horse's obedience and suppleness; a speed and endurance section which involves a cross country ride to test the horse's speed, stamina and jumping ability over fixed, imposing fences; and finally a show jumping round to illustrate that the horse is still fit and sound after the rigours of the cross country.

Eventing has become increasingly popular in recent years with large numbers of people competing at all levels. It also draws huge crowds of spectators, particularly for major events like the Whitbread Championships at Badminton in England, regarded as the world's premier event.

Affiliated events, which are run under the auspices of each country's governing body, may be run over one to four days, depending on the level of the competition.

The highest level is the Three Day Event — although the name is a little misleading as the competition actually takes four days! The reason for the discrepancy is that the first phase, the dressage, usually takes two days for all the horses in the competition to complete. Many Riding and Pony Clubs hold one day events when all three phases are completed on the same day.

For affiliated horse trials the horses have to progress through novice, intermediate and advanced competitions, gaining points along the way according to their placings.

Below: The supreme challenge of horse and rider lies in eventing, with the Badminton Horse Trials in Britain the premier competition. The famous Lake fences threaten the unlucky with a ducking.

Ordinary horse owners or the general public who visit top class events such as Badminton and Burghley never cease to be astounded by the courage and skill of the event riders and their horses.

At this level, during the speed and endurance day, riders have to complete a steeplechase course (phase B) and two phases (A and C) of roads and tracks work, before tackling the fourth phase (D) — the cross country

FACT FILE

●The governing body for eventing in Britain is the British Horse Society Horse Trials Group.

●In the USA, eventing is run by the United States Combined Training Association.

●Important US eventing competitions include the Rolex Kentucky Three Day Event in Lexington, Kentucky, and the Radnor Hunt Three Day Event in Radnor, Pennsylvania.

course, which is usually four to four and a half miles (about 6.5-7km). The courses make use of natural features such as hedges, ditches, stone walls, drops and banks and, although the height limit for fences is 3ft 11in (120cm), they can look almost unjumpable! Eventing is definitely not a sport for the faint-hearted. For instance, Badminton competitors make little of jumping over the Whitbread Drays — the actual vehicles which Shires can be seen pulling!

At the start of a three day event all the horses are vetted by a panel of veterinary surgeons. On speed and endurance day there is a ten minute rest between finishing phase C and starting D (the cross country course) when the vets also check the horses over. On the final day, there is another veterinary inspection before the show jumping. Horses which are not sound are withdrawn or 'spun' by the veterinary panel.

In the show jumping round, unlike in ordinary show jumping competitions, any mistake made by the horse and rider is marked in penalty points rather than faults.

At the end of all three phases of horse trials, whether it is a major three day event or an unaffiliated riding club occasion, the rider with the lowest number of penalty points is the winner.

Rodeos

Rodeos are sporting events which are also incredibly exciting spectacles. The sight of brightly attired cowboys riding bucking broncos, roping calves or riding bulls attracts large, enthusiastic audiences.

The Spanish introduced cattle and horses to America, and the word rodeo comes from the Spanish for 'round-up'. Early settlers originally bred cattle and horses for their own use but the coming of the railways opened up the markets of the growing towns. Cowboys drove the cattle to rail junctions, holding contests of everyday skills to pass the time before the train's arrival.

At the beginning of this century cowboy competitions became attractions at horse shows and fairs. The professional rodeo cowboy was about to be born as ranch hands could earn far more in a few seconds at a show than during weeks on a ranch.

By 1945 the Rodeo Cowboys' Association had drawn up rules and safety regulations, and had organized the sport to better advantage. Since then rodeos have grown, attracting both contestants and spectators with off-shoots such as rodeo schools and leagues in high schools and colleges.

Above: Competitions demonstrating cowboy skills, such as calf roping, are popular attractions at Canada's Calgary Stampede and feature in rodeos throughout the USA.

Hunting

Man has always hunted — initially for food — one of the reasons horses were domesticated was that they made hunting easier.

In Britain, hunting is a part of the nation's heritage, with packs of hounds being used to track down quarry as long ago as the 11th century. Although the main quarry used to be stags and hares, by the 18th century attention turned to the fox.

Hunting is an autumn/winter sport carried out in Britain, Europe and America, although the fact that it is a blood sport appals some people. As an alternative there is draghunting which offers all the thrills of a fast ride across country, jumping whatever obstacle is in the way, with the hounds following a trail laid by runners.

The hounds lead the hunt, accompanied by the hunt officials known as the Huntsman and the Whippers-in. The riders who are following the hunt are known as the field and are under the charge of the Field Master. Overall responsibility for the hunt belongs to the person appointed as Master.

Below: The sight of huntsmen and hounds is part of the British heritage and has spread to other countries. Draghunting provides the thrill of the chase without a kill.

Hunter Trials

These usually take place over farmland and consist of a course of fixed jumps over a distance of about 2.5km (1½ miles). They are designed to test the horse's speed, jumping ability and handiness. To illustrate the latter, many hunter trial courses include a gate which has to be opened and closed as part of the timed section.

FACT FILE

- In 1742 two Irishmen settled a bet by racing their hunters four miles between church steeples — the first steeplechase.

- The English turf Classics are the 2000 Guineas (colts), 1000 Guineas (fillies), Derby, Oaks and St Leger.

- The US Triple Crown consists of the Belmont Stakes (1867), the Preakness (1873) and the Kentucky Derby (1875).

- European flat racing is on grass, from early March to early November. US racing is all year round, on dirt.

Some events time the horse and rider around the whole course, others designate a section of the course as the part where time plays a deciding factor. The majority of the jumps at these events are natural ones such as ditches, walls and hedges, although some are man-made, with rustic poles rather than brightly coloured poles.

Often hunter trials are run by the local hunt, Pony Club or Riding Club. There are usually classes for individuals and for pairs.

Long Distance Riding

Of all the equestrian disciplines long distance riding must have the earliest origins, for Man has been using the horse to cover large distances for centuries — whether in hunts for food, as mounts for battles, as pack horses or a means of carrying the mail. Yet the sport of long distance riding did not come into being until the turn of this century, with some European countries holding some demanding and tragic rides. As a result of one 400-mile (about 650km) race, 25 horses lost their lives.

Although there were some endurance and pleasure rides in Great Britain in the 1920s and '30s, it was not until the mid-60s that the impetus which has made long distance riding a blossoming sport, began. Britain's most famous event is the Golden Horseshoe

Ride, while the USA has the Tevis Cup ride, first held in 1955, and Australia organizes the Tom Quilty Endurance Ride, launched in 1966. Long distance riding is also enjoyed in Europe and New Zealand.

This sport entails horse and rider covering a set number of miles at a set speed. The distance and speed varies according to the level of the competition. For instance, riders can start to enjoy the sport by joining pleasure rides of 15 miles (about 25km) with a minimum speed of 5mph.

They may progress to competitive trail rides where the distances vary from 25-60 miles (40-90km). In an open competition the rider would need to maintain an average speed of between 7 and 8mph (11 and 13km/h). This may sound relatively easy but it must be remembered that horse and rider are covering all kinds of terrain — negotiating rivers, streams, steep slopes, roads, mountain tracks and so on.

The skill lies in producing a horse and rider fit enough to cope with the demands of the ride. Before and after each ride the horses have to be vetted — any horse which is not sound is not allowed to compete or is 'spun' out of the competition. In longer rides the vets are out on the course and can pull a horse up if they are concerned about his fitness, condition or soundness.

Endurance rides are at the highest level of this sport — usually they cover 100 miles (160km), perhaps over 24 hours or split into two days of 50 miles (80km) per day. During longer rides there are statutory halts when vets again examine the horses.

Racing

Racing horses has been a popular pastime since Man first domesticated the horse and today it is a thriving industry in many countries. It is not surprising that the sport originated in 17th century Britain where its development coincided with the development of the Thoroughbred.

There had been some form of racing in Britain since the arrival of the Romans but it was not until the time of the Restoration (1660-88), when King Charles II was restored to the throne, that racing started to take major steps forward. Previously races had been held between two horses, but the King encouraged larger fields by offering prizes.

Left: *Both horse and rider are tackling this fixed fence boldly. Positive riding is needed over hunter trial fences, especially when there are ditches behind, as here.*

In addition to organizing the races the King rode in them as well. Racing at this time involved three or four heats of four-mile gallops. As the Thoroughbred developed, interest in racing grew.

In 1750 another major event happened: a group of sportsmen formed the Jockey Club based at Newmarket. Originally it was intended that the club should regulate racing at its own centre but, in time, its control spread to courses throughout Britain.

Horses were being raced at an earlier age and a series of races, the Classics, was started to establish which of the three-year-olds each season were the ideal Thoroughbreds.

In the United States racing developed with the emergence of the Quarter Horse. Colonists in the Eastern states raced horses in towns, usually over a quarter-mile distance. The first Thoroughbred was imported from Britain in 1700, and by the late 18th century flat racing over longer courses was established. An American jockey, Willie Sims, introduced the modern crouched race-riding style, with shortened reins and short stirrups, in 1895.

Below: Water obstacles are just one of the many challenges to be found in combined driving which tests the skill and resourcefulness of both horses and driver.

Above: Flat racing has become a major sport in many countries. On American tracks, such as this Miami course, the horses race on dirt rather than grass.

Racing today is a truly international sport, with race-meetings held across the world. The United States, Britain, France, Italy, Australia, New Zealand and Japan are just some of the major racing countries.

Horses have proved their worth over jumps as well as on the flat, but although steeplechasing and point-to-pointing have a huge following in Britain they will never have the same appeal as flat racing as they do not support a major breeding industry. Many of the jump racing horses are geldings (neutered males) and, as the horses are raced later in their lives than are flat racing horses (at 10 or 11 years of age), even the successful jump mares will not have such long stud careers as their flat racing sisters.

Driving

Another of the growing equestrian sports is that of driving. The vehicles are driven, not raced, and many people drive simply for pleasure, perhaps breaking a favourite pony to harness so that he can continue to lead a useful life. Yet once people get the driving bug they often take up driving as a sport. This may take the form of the glamour and prestige of show driving or the skill and resourcefulness of combined driving.

Show driving requires quality horses with good conformation, action and manners, combined with immaculate turn-out of the

horse, driver, carriage and occupants. Often there are classes open to particular breeds, such as Hackneys and Welsh Cobs.

Combined driving has increased in popularity in recent years with the success and involvement of HRH The Duke of Edinburgh bringing the sport to the public eye. Presentation, dressage, marathon and obstacle driving are all part of the competition in combined driving.

Harness Racing

The modern world has its own version of chariot racing in the guise of harness racing. In ancient times the horses were galloped in the races but now trotting is the required pace. Nevertheless, the races are still very demanding and strenuous for the horses.

Harness racing is enjoyed throughout the world with the races taking place on hard or grass tracks. Usually the distance covered is a mile and if the horses break into a canter or gallop they are penalized. Behind them the horses pull a carriage, in which their driver sits, with his legs apart and his feet firmly placed in fixed stirrups.

Names for the carriage vary from country to country as do the rules for harness racing. The only universal rule is that trotting is the only pace allowed. In America and Australia the carriage is known as a sulky, in Britain it is a cart, and in other countries it is known as a buggy or bike.

There are two types of horses used as there are two types of gait allowed; trotters move their legs in diagonal pairs, while pacers trot with both legs on one side moving together.

Above: *The Red Mile, Kentucky — although harness racers may only trot, they build up considerable speed, providing an exciting spectacle for racegoers.*

Mounted Games

For many people mounted games means the sight of Pony Club teams of young riders and their ponies twisting through poles, the riders vaulting on and off with ease, the ponies stopping and turning on a coin. This is also known as gymkhana, which means a 'field day on horseback'.

Games on horseback cover a wide spectrum. They are designed to test the rider's control, athleticism, co-ordination and boldness whilst the pony is required to be forward-going, fast, obedient and supple.

Mounted Games are played by children all over the world yet their origins lie in the adult equestrian world and with a far more serious purpose.

Since Man has been riding he has been keen to show off his skills on horseback. In the Middle Ages the noblemen who were not at war spent their time keeping themselves and their horses prepared for combat by jousting. Eventually jousting tournaments changed from being serious contests which often claimed the lives of knights to spectator sports. Special rules — the code of chivalry — were drawn up for the contests run in England, France and Germany.

In the mid to late 19th century British Army personnel serving in India organized games on horseback to keep themselves amused and to improve their riding skills.

Polo

Although polo has the image of being the sport of princes and very much a 'rich man's game', many young people play at Pony Club level. It is a very exciting and fast game to watch, with spectators thrilled by the skill and control of the players and the agility, speed and courage of their ponies. The sport originated over two thousand years ago

Above: *Mounted games riders need to be totally confident and at one with their ponies, especially if they are to perform tasks such as this, mounted on a pony that is cantering and ready to turn.*

in Persia and was introduced into Britain in the 19th century. It is now a world-wide sport with associations in countries such as the USA, Britain, Argentina, Australia, Malaysia and Africa.

The game consists of two opposing teams, each with four mounted members, trying to score as many goals as possible using mallets and a small wooden ball. Players are handicapped according to their ability. Games are divided into 'chukkas' which last seven minutes. A full match will have six chukkas with three minutes in between each chukka to enable players to change their ponies. No pony is allowed to play more than two chukkas per game and is not ridden for two consecutive chukkas.

As this is a very physical game both ponies and riders wear protective clothing. Although still referred to as polo *ponies,* the mounts can, in fact, be over 14.2 hands, with the average height at around 15 hands.

The game is umpired by two mounted riders who are usually experienced players themselves.

Showing

Showing is basically the art of presenting your horse in the best possible way so that it catches the eye of the judges and, hopefully, impresses them so much that you are awarded a prize!

The range of show classes varies a great deal according to which country you are in. Often the indigenous breeds of the country are displayed, for instance the Mountain and Moorland breeds in Britain, or the American Saddlebred and Morgans of the USA.

Many horses are very versatile and this has to be reflected in the range of classes available to them — for instance in America Morgans can compete as parade horses; pleasure horses; working hunters; jumpers; trail horses and cutting horses.

The American Horse Shows Association has a Hunter Division which is again subdivided so that, for owners of Working Hunters, there are thirty possible classes.

Although the perfect horse does not exist, show animals should be superb examples of their breed or type. Their conformation — that is, their structure and shape — will be examined by the judges, as will their

Right: During a horse show, the extravagant paces of a Welsh Cob are demonstrated. The handler must keep up with the horse in order that the cob can be shown to the best advantage in front of the judges.

Below: In the fast-moving world of polo, HRH the Prince of Wales is recognized as a highly skilful player. All polo players must be tough and experienced riders.

action — the way the horse moves. A horse must be well proportioned and pleasing, with a free, straight and rhythmical action.

The manners of the horse are also taken into account, especially children's ridden pony and riding horse classes.

Before a horse or pony is taken into the show ring a great deal of preparation is necessary. Good management in terms of exercise, feeding and grooming is needed to ensure the animal is fit, healthy and in good condition to be presented in the ring.

Various manoeuvres should also have been practised before a horse enters the ring, such as running the horse up in hand and standing square. The handler runs alongside, encouraging him to show off his paces and to stand with front and hind legs properly positioned in line. Some classes require the horse and rider to give an individual show including changes of paces, circles and halts to show that the horse is obedient, supple and responsive.

Some classes require the horse's mane and tail to be plaited (braided) while others insist on the horse being left natural with a full, unpulled mane and tail. (Pulling involves thinning out and shortening the mane.) The rider's turnout should match the high standards of the horse's appearance; different classes require different riding clothes.

PART TWO

POPULAR BREEDS OF HORSES AND PONIES

There are many different breeds of horses and ponies in the world, over 35 of which are featured in this section. A breed is a group of horses which have similar physical attributes and conform to certain conditions with regards to height and colour. Some breeds, such as the Camargue, have evolved naturally and can live quite happily in the wild, being well adapted to their environment. Others, such as the Thoroughbred, have been 'engineered' by Man and developed through cross-breeding. Such 'man-made' breeds are often more dependent on humans for their food, shelter and warmth. The breeds in this section have been divided according to their region of origin, with the exception of the Arab and Thoroughbred — these are such outstanding horses, and have been used so extensively in the development of other breeds, that each has been granted a chapter of its own.

Left: Fast, elegant and athletic, Thoroughbreds are regarded as the classic racehorse. They are widely used in breeding to improve other breeds of horse.

POINTS, COLOURS AND MARKINGS

POINTS OF A HORSE

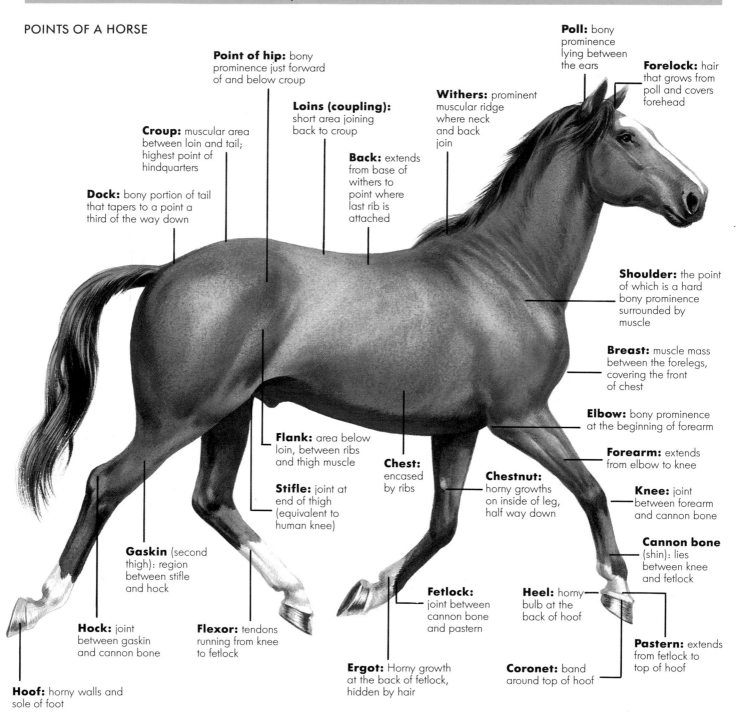

Point of hip: bony prominence just forward of and below croup

Loins (coupling): short area joining back to croup

Croup: muscular area between loin and tail; highest point of hindquarters

Back: extends from base of withers to point where last rib is attached

Dock: bony portion of tail that tapers to a point a third of the way down

Withers: prominent muscular ridge where neck and back join

Poll: bony prominence lying between the ears

Forelock: hair that grows from poll and covers forehead

Shoulder: the point of which is a hard bony prominence surrounded by muscle

Breast: muscle mass between the forelegs, covering the front of chest

Elbow: bony prominence at the beginning of forearm

Forearm: extends from elbow to knee

Flank: area below loin, between ribs and thigh muscle

Stifle: joint at end of thigh (equivalent to human knee)

Chest: encased by ribs

Chestnut: horny growths on inside of leg, half way down

Knee: joint between forearm and cannon bone

Cannon bone (shin): lies between knee and fetlock

Gaskin (second thigh): region between stifle and hock

Hock: joint between gaskin and cannon bone

Flexor: tendons running from knee to fetlock

Fetlock: joint between cannon bone and pastern

Heel: horny bulb at the back of hoof

Pastern: extends from fetlock to top of hoof

Ergot: Horny growth at the back of fetlock, hidden by hair

Coronet: band around top of hoof

Hoof: horny walls and sole of foot

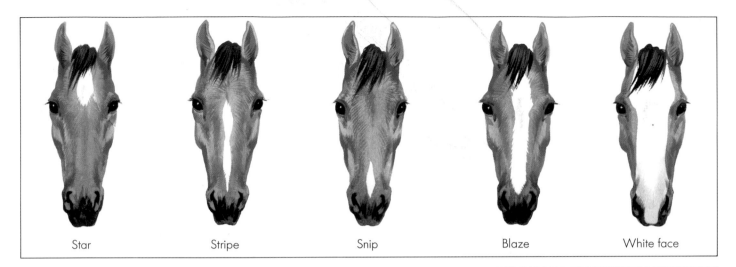

| Star | Stripe | Snip | Blaze | White face |

Many references to horses on height, markings and veterinary matters relate to various parts — or points — of the horse's body, so it is useful to know some of the more common ones (see opposite).

The height of a horse or pony is measured in hands, each hand being the equivalent to four inches (10cm). The measurement is taken from the ground to the withers — the prominent ridge where the neck and back join. Fractions of height are expressed in inches, for example, 14.2 hands means 14 hands and two inches. Ponies measure up to 14.2 hands and anything over this is a horse.

There are many different colours of horses and a few unfounded superstitions relating to certain ones. For instance, some people are loathe to have a chestnut mare as mares of this colour are supposed to have a fiery temperament!

The four main coat colours are black, brown, bay and chestnut, other colours being modifications of these four (see right for descriptions of colours). White is not a colour and indicates a lack of pigmentation (colouration). To establish a horse's colour you should look at the points, meaning the muzzle, legs, mane, tail and tips of ears.

Foals may not necessarily remain the colour they are born but, although there are some exceptions, they usually achieve their adult colour by the age of two.

Distinctive white markings on a horse's face are described using various terms. A star is a white mark of any shape on the forehead; a stripe is a narrow white line which runs down the face; a snip is a small white mark on or between the nostrils; a blaze is a broad band of white that runs from the forehead to the nose; and a white face is a broader version of a blaze which usually includes the forehead, eyes, nose and part of the muzzle. The leg markings are shown below.

COLOURS OF A HORSE

Black A black coat and points with no other colours except perhaps white markings on the face or legs.

Brown A brown coat and points; white markings are allowed on the face or legs.

Bay A brown coat with black points; the coat colour may range from light to dark.

Chestnut A bright reddish-brown coat which may range from light to dark; the points may be a shade lighter or darker than the coat but never black.

Grey A mixture of white and black hairs throughout the coat; may range from light to dark and the coat usually becomes whiter with age.

Dun The coat may vary from a mousey colour to a golden yellow; points are black and there may be a stripe down the back and zebra markings on the legs.

Roan A mixture of two hair colours in the coat, one of which is white, eg. chestnut and white hairs produce a strawberry roan.

Leg markings are usually named after the part of the leg which they affect, such as the pastern or coronet. In a stocking, white extends from the coronet to the knee or hock; socks reach half way up the cannon bone.

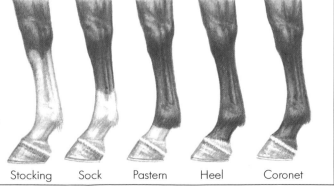

| Stocking | Sock | Pastern | Heel | Coronet |

THE ARAB

The Arab, the oldest pure breed of horse in the world, has exerted a tremendous influence over many other breeds of horses and ponies. From Morgans in the USA to Akhal-Teke in the USSR, Welsh Mountain ponies in Britain to Criollos in Argentina, the wide-ranging influence of the Arabian horse can be seen.

The Arab's established position of supremacy in the horse world has been possible because of the purity of its breed; it has been selectively bred — that is, bred from the finest samples of its type — for over a thousand years longer than any other breed. It also has a greater ability than other breeds to stamp its qualities on its offspring.

Bedouins, the nomadic tribes of the Arabian deserts whose name is virtually synonymous with the breed, jealously guarded the purity of their desert horses. No other breed was allowed to sully the Arab's blood and the selective breeding ensured that only supremely tough, enduring, high quality animals were produced.

In addition, the Islamic religion promoted the keeping of horses as part of the faith and in the 7th century AD the prophet Mohammed raised the status of the Arab horse by telling his people that paradise awaited those who cared for their horses.

As Moslem cavalries left their homelands and began to conquer new lands, the Arab horse came into contact with other breeds. In this way, its immense influence on the development of other equines began.

Arabs are renowned for their love of human company — and the origins of this lie in their long association with the Bed-

Below: The Arab is a magnificent horse which has influenced many other breeds, such as the Morgan and the Welsh Mountain Pony.

Left: *An Arab horse and rider dressed in traditional Bedouin costume. The prophet Mohammed, founder of the Moslem religion, taught that the Arab horse was created by Allah.*

Below: *Arabs are shown with their silky manes and tails left natural, that is, not plaited. This enhances the sheer grace and elegance of the breed.*

ouin tribes, the major breeders of the original Arabs. These tribes people hand-fed their horses and even had their Arabs sleeping in their tents with them! Although the desert conditions meant only the fittest and strongest survived, the ever constant human element present in the Arab's history ensured the breed maintained a docile nature.

According to Bedouin legend, all Arabs are descended from a mare owned by Baz (3000 BC), the great-great grandson of Noah, and a stallion called Hoshaba. Legend also has it that the Arab was created by God from the South Wind, hence the horse's great speed, which made it so admired. Solomon, King of Israel, captured Arabs in Egypt and is believed to have had 1,200 riding horses and 40,000 chariot horses in his stables.

Details of Arab breeding were handed down by word of mouth from generation to generation of desert people. The Bedouin breeding policy ensured the breed displayed qualities of stamina, soundness, speed, courage, dignity and beauty as well as being able to carry weights out of proportion to its size for long periods.

The Bedouins selected the stallions according to their intelligence, conformation and beauty, whilst the mares were chosen for their stamina. Mares were also put to rigorous tests, being used both in battle and for hunting.

Throughout the centuries poets and artists have celebrated the beauty of this magnificent horse, whilst tales of the Arab's outstanding courage and endurance in war have enthralled many a listener.

The Arab is typified by its short, refined, and dished head, large, widely spaced eyes, small, soft muzzle with large nostrils and small, shapely ears. It has long sloping shoulders, a short back, generous hindquarters and a deep girth. The limbs are strong and hard with dense bones, and the mane and tail are fine and silky. The tail is carried high and arched. Characteristically, Arabs should have near perfect feet.

Although usually standing between 14.1 and 15.2 hands, the Arab's balance and action means that the horses tend to feel bigger. Their action is unique; Arabs have a very free expressive action, moving lightly and easily over the ground as if floating. Chestnut and bay were the original colours of the breed but now it may be any solid colour, grey being particularly popular.

Many famous lines of Arabians are spread all over the world and there is hardly any country which does not have important Arab stock. Two of the oldest lines are the Persian and the Egyptian. The latter was greatly promoted by Abbas Pasha, Viceroy of Egypt between 1848 and 1850, and his horses are the ancestors of some of the finest breeds found today in the United States, Britain and Egypt.

Other famous Arab lines include that in Britain which is based on early stock brought over soon after the Crusades. Poland, too, has an old and pure line of Arabs.

FACT FILE

● Arabs often have only 17 pairs of ribs instead of the usual 18 or 19; five lumbar vertebrae instead of six and 16 tail vertebrae instead of 18.

● Arab horses are depicted in Ancient Egyptian art, 3000 years old.

● Arabs are sometimes called 'Drinkers of the Wind' because of their speed.

● In the Koran, the Muslim holy book, horses are called the 'supreme blessing'.

THE THOROUGHBRED

Looked upon as the 'super horse', the Thoroughbred is the fastest breed in the world and is the most highly esteemed. It has taken less than 200 years to develop this breed and, although other imported Arabian sires have also played their part in the horse's history, all of today's Thoroughbreds can trace their ancestry to three Arabian foundation sires imported into Britain during the late 17th and early 18th century.

The first to arrive was the Byerley Turk, named after his captor, Captain Robert Byerley, who fought in Hungary against the Turkish invaders. This lovely Arab was used as a charger for several years before being sent to stand at stud in the north of England, where he was used on a wide range of British racing mares.

The Darley Arabian, the second of the three foundation sires, was bought as a four-year-old by Thomas Darley, British Consul in Aleppo. The horse had been bred on the edge of the Syrian desert and, upon moving to Britain in 1704, proved to be a very successful sire. One of his progeny was the first top-class racehorse, Flying Childers, and in later years the Darley Arabian line included Eclipse, one of the greatest racehorses of all time.

Above: The ultimate equine racing machine, the Thoroughbred thrills enthusiasts all over the world, racing on turf, dirt and even on snow!

Below: Originally bred for the flat, the Thoroughbred's jumping skills have led to its supremacy in other racing spheres, such as the Grand National steeplechase in Britain.

Last but not least was the Godolphin Arabian, who was born in the Yemen and, as a nine-year-old, became the property of Lord Godolphin. The horse's origins are rather obscure and there is a story that he once pulled a cart in the streets of Paris. However, the stallion was sent to stud near Cambridge. His progeny include Matchem who, like Eclipse, was to found an outstanding male line.

By the time the foundation sires arrived in England, the racing of horses was already well established, with native mares being crossed with imported Arabs, Barbs and Turks. However, it was not until after the introduction of these sires that breeders started to test their stock, putting them on the racecourse so they could prove themselves.

To establish and improve a breed it is necessary to keep records of pedigrees and performances and by 1791 the first of Weatherby's General Stud Books appeared. Nowadays, only animals entered in the GSB are eligible to compete in races.

At this point racehorses were only around 14.2 hands. Although a definite pattern for the Thoroughbred had emerged, trends were changing in that the breeders were aiming for bigger, faster horses, able to compete at a younger age. By the 19th century the Thoroughbred averaged 16 hands and records on the racetrack were consistently being broken.

These elegant, long-legged horses with their tremendous presence, quality and stamina were soon being imported into other lands. Only fifty years after the Byerley Turk's arrival, Thoroughbreds were being taken to America by settlers. From these horses the rich American racing industry has evolved with the famous 'blue grass' country of Kentucky being a highly successful breeding area.

Although originally bred for flat-racing, Thoroughbreds have proved themselves in many other spheres. Within the racing world they can also jump at speed, as witnessed in steeplechases. They also dominate the world of eventing (see page 28).

Below: *The Thoroughbred averages 16 hands and is found in most solid colours. Breeding Thoroughbreds is a worldwide industry.*

FACT FILE

• The Thoroughbred is the fastest and most valuable breed in the world.

• They have perhaps the most perfect conformation of all horses.

• Many of the mares served by the Thoroughbred's founding sires were of oriental or part-oriental blood.

AMERICAN BREEDS

Although the ancestors of today's horses are known to have originated in North America, the continent's horse population was wiped out about ten thousand years ago. No-one knows why this happened.

The modern American horse population owes its existence to the Spanish conquistadores who came to the 'New World' in the 15th century. One of the most famous of these soldier adventurers was Hernando Cortez who conquered Mexico (1519-21). His name is mentioned later in connection with Palominos and Pinto horses.

As Spain started to explore the American continent, the King of Spain decreed that all ships sailing to the New World should include 12 mares so that new stocks of horses could be built up. The native Indians were terrified of the creatures at first; when the Spanish fired their guns the Indians believed the horses were the source of the gunfire.

Below: A group of Appaloosas. Appaloosas have eight basic patterns of coat and no two animals have the same markings.

When some of the Spanish horses escaped, herds developed in the wild, and it is from these early horses that many American breeds are derived. The Indians, for example, soon lost their fears and began to breed horses for their own purposes. Later, when the West was opened up, the new settlers and cattlemen also used this vast stock of wild horses to develop new breeds.

APPALOOSA

Noted for its spots, the Appaloosa is one of America's foremost breeds and is now found in many countries of the world. Although there are other spotted horses — some are even depicted in prehistoric cave drawings — the true Appaloosa can be distinguished by the grey-pink mottled skin around its nostrils, lips and genitalia and the white area or sclera around the iris of the eye. The horse measures over 14.2 hands and usually has a wispy mane and tail.

A North American Indian tribe, the Nez Perce, have the strongest links with this breed. Spotted horses are believed to have been introduced into America by the Spanish around 1600. The Indians took some to their homelands near the Palouse river and bred them for their strength, speed and stamina. These horses became known by the French as 'A Palouse', which eventually became Appaloosa.

When the Nez Perce surrendered to the US Army in 1877, the Indian horses were either sold or turned free. Luckily, the breed was saved thanks to the hard work of Oregon's Claude Thomson. He started a selective breeding programme, introducing Arab blood to restore quality to the breed. The Appaloosa Horse Club of America has been in existence since 1938.

They had with them their Arabs, Morgans and Plantation horses and it is from these horses that a fast riding horse for cowboys, ranchers and sheriffs was developed. Doctors also rode them on their rounds.

A distinctive feature of this breed is their fox trotting gait — the horse walks in front and trots behind. This makes for a comfortable ride and the horse is as much in demand now as it was when first founded.

Other attractive features of Missouri Fox Trotters are their docility and ease of handling. Very much a pleasure horse, the Fox Trotter is noted for its sure-footedness and so is useful for endurance riding.

FACT FILE

- Appaloosa foals are born with coats of uniform colour. The markings appear later.

- The stallion Justin Morgan was originally called Figure. He came into the ownership of the Vermont teacher as settlement of a debt.

- Missouri Fox Trotters can reach up to 16km/h (10mph) with their unusual gait.

MORGAN HORSE

The Morgan is unusual in that, whereas most breeds evolve over a period of time, this breed came about in just one generation. In America in the 1790s, a great deal of land was being cleared so that homes could be built. To supplement his income, a Vermont schoolteacher used his stallion to pull logs, which the horse, named Justin Morgan after his owner, did with ease, outpulling all his rivals. When raced, both under saddle and in harness, the horse was equally successful and soon the stallion was in great demand as a sire. Whatever type of mare, Justin's progeny were stamped with their sire's qualities.

The breed became known as Morgans and have since influenced other breeds such as the American Saddlebred, Standardbred and Tennessee Walking Horse.

Stunning paces, speed, stamina, a kind docile temperament and great presence were qualities which Justin Morgan possessed and which Morgans are now famous for. They have a robust but refined conformation.

MISSOURI FOX TROTTER

The need for a horse which was fast and comfortable to ride for long distances resulted in the formation of the Missouri Fox Trotter breed. It was founded in the early 1800s by pioneers who settled in Missouri.

Above: *Morgans present a picture of elegance, yet they have excellent powers of endurance and are economical to keep.*

Below: *One of the most comfortable rides is given by the Missouri Fox Trotter, which is very popular for trail riding.*

Below: The wiry Mustangs are part of the heritage of America's Wild West — tough, clever and brave.

MUSTANGS

Mustangs are the original horses of the Wild West, tough brave creatures descended from the Andalusian and Barb horses taken to North America by the Spanish.

When some of the early horses escaped from the Spanish they ran free and multiplied to form great wild herds. These early Mustangs were good representatives of the elegant Spanish stock, but the best of them were taken by the Indians who used them for hunting bison, or caught by the cowboys for working livestock.

As the wild herds were continually robbed of the best animals, so the quality of the Mustangs declined. At the same time, the settlers were moving West, using their riding and carriage horses to cross with the wiry Mustangs. As a result, the true Mustang became virtually crossbred to extinction. And those horses that were still roaming free by the turn of the century were rounded up and either shot or sold because they were considered a nuisance by cattle ranchers.

The original mounts of the American cowboy, Mustangs are still used in rodeos (see page 29). They may be any colour and usually stand between 13.2 and 15 hands. To-day, attempts are being made to preserve Mustangs of the pure Barb type and several registries have been set up in the USA.

PALOMINO

Palominos are not recognized as a breed but as a colour; their coats are golden whilst the mane and tail are white-blond. With this striking colour combination it is not surprising that they are known as the 'Golden Horse of the West'.

The coat colour can be various shades of gold, from a creamy colour to a dark chestnut. The mane and tail must have no more than 15% dark or chestnut hair in them. White markings are allowed on the face and below the knee.

Although no-one knows when this coat colour first appeared it is thought to be one of the early colours. The French Bayeux Tapestry of the 11th century depicts what appear to be golden coated horses, and early Chinese emperors were said to ride golden horses with silver manes and tails.

Palominos are relatives of the Arab and Barb, and were once known as Isabellas. This

name dates from the 15th century and was in honour of Queen Isabella of Spain who was a keen supporter of the breed. The Queen presented some to Count de Palomino who is believed to have named them after himself. Another explanation, however, for their name is that they were named after the golden palomino grape.

The explorer Cortez took some 'Golden Isabellas' to Mexico in the early 1500s, but many of the horses escaped and joined up with herds of Mustangs in the wild. They later became very popular with the American cowboys who captured the handsome horses and trained them as cow ponies.

Today, Palominos are bred across the world. As they are a colour rather than a breed, their conformation and temperament vary according to the type. Breeds accepted vary from country to country, those in the USA including the Saddlebred and the

Right: *As well as being remarkable sprinters, Quarter Horses have a talent for working with cattle. They seem to have an innate ability to predict how a cow will behave.*

Below: *With its stunning colours, the Palomino makes a striking sight in show classes.*

Quarter Horse. Palominos do not breed true and if two Palominos mate there is no guarantee that the foal will be Palomino.

These horses may be any height and can be found in all kinds of equestrian sports, from driving and long distance riding to Western riding and jumping.

QUARTER HORSE

Quarter Horses are superb sprinting machines able to cover short distances at fantastic speeds from standing starts. Quarter Horse racing is run over distances of 220-440 yds (about 200-400m) with most horses clocking speeds of 40mph and top USA champions reaching 45mph.

The horses were developed in the 17th century by English settlers in Virginia, and North and South Carolina. By crossing quick-witted Indian ponies (who had Spanish ancestry) with imported Thoroughbreds the 'Illustrious Colonial Quarter of a Mile Running Horse' was born.

The founding sire was an English Thoroughbred called Janus who was a grandson of the Godolphin Arabian and raced successfully over distances of four miles. However, his progeny ran at their best over the quarter-mile sprints, hence the name Quarter Horse.

By day these early Quarter Horses worked on the plantations of the South and at weekends they raced down the main streets of the towns. Now, Quarter Horse racing is a multi-million dollar business in the USA and its popularity is growing in Great Britain where it is run along the same lines as Thoroughbred race meetings. The Jockey Club oversees Quarter Horse racing in the United Kingdom.

Quarter Horses have very strong hindquarters, backs and loins which gives them the propulsive power and strength for the demands of racing. They have a heavy frame but a compact, muscular body.

Quarter Horses proved strong enough to carry heavy riders all day. With the spread of cattle ranches, they became known as the best cow ponies, and later as rodeo horses. Quarter Horses remain in great demand as cow ponies as they have not only the speed, but the ability to twist and turn sharply as they work the cattle and single out an animal from the herds.

Despite their razor sharp reactions, great speed and strength, these horses have very calm natures and are also represented in general leisure riding and showing. The usual colour for the Quarter Horse is chestnut although any solid colour is acceptable. In height they stand 15.1 to 16.1 hands.

PINTO

Like the Palomino (page 44), the Pinto is a colour type rather than a true breed. It was among the first horses taken to South America by the Spanish explorer Cortez, and is also known as the Paint horse in America, although in Europe and Asia such horses are called coloured horses.

In many people's minds Pintos are linked with the North American Indians. The Indians certainly favoured these horses because they were hardy creatures and their colouring acted as camouflage. There are two types of colouring: black with white patches (called piebald in Britain) and white with brown or bay patches (known as skewbald in Britain).

The pattern of the coat also varies. *Overos* have white patches starting from the belly and extending upwards, a dark mane, back and tail, and a white face. *Tobianos* tend to have larger white patches that start on the back, at least one white front leg with white extending over the shoulders and withers, and head markings like those of a solid coloured horse — that is, the head should be all one colour or have a white blaze, stripe, star or snip on the face.

As Pintos can be seen among many breeds, their conformation and temperament vary. In the United States, Pintos are covered by three separate registries, including the Pinto Registry started in 1956. In Britain, they are registered by the Coloured Horse and Pony Society, founded in 1983.

Below: *Colour genes (factors of inheritance) in true Pintos are so strong that it is rare for a solid-coloured foal to be born to Pinto parents.*

Below: *The American Standardbred has proved so good as a harness racing horse that it has been exported all over the world to improve other breeds of harness racer.*

FACT FILE

- Pinto derives from the Spanish word meaning painted.

- No two Pinto or paint horses carry the same markings.

- The unique gaits of Walking Horses are natural, and foals execute them without any training. Both gaits are four-time movements.

AMERICAN STANDARDBRED

Reputed to be the world's fastest horse for harness racing, this breed derives its name from the 'time standard' introduced to test the ability of harness racers before they were eligible for the American Trotter Register.

Although their name dates from 1879, the American Standardbred originated 200 years ago with the official foundation sire being

Above: The running walk of the Tennessee Walking Horse is a faster version of the flat-foot walk. The high, rolling canter is just as comfortable for the rider.

an English Thoroughbred called Messenger who was a descendant of the Darley Arabian. Despite other blood such as Morgan and Norfolk Trotter being introduced, almost all Standardbreds can be traced back to four sons of Hambletonian, a descendant of Messenger.

Originally, the horses were used for informal trotting races but by the 19th century these had become increasingly official harness races. Selective breeding to produce even faster horses resulted, and by the 1870s there was a Trotter Register. The standard imposed for entry to this was a one-mile-speed of two and a half minutes for trotters and two minutes 25 seconds for pacers. Since then the entry standards have been altered and now relate to blood alone.

Standardbreds may trot or pace, that is, move their legs in lateral rather than diagonal pairs. If they show a tendency for pacing at an early age they are trained in that gait.

These horses are so good as harness racers that they have been used to improve other breeds all over the world, such as the Orlov Trotters. They are bred on a large scale in the United States for harness racing.

TENNESSEE WALKING HORSE

This breed was developed in the 19th century in the Southern States of America to carry riders on inspection tours of the large plantations. Originally it was known as the Plantation Walking or 'turn row' horse because the overseers could ride between the rows without the horse causing any damage to the crops.

In addition to the normal paces Tennessee Walking Horses have three unique gaits: the flat foot walk, running walk and a 'rocking horse' canter. Their running walk enables them to reach speeds in excess of 13km/h (8mph), yet they are extremely comfortable to ride as they move their legs from the elbow rather than the shoulder.

Morgan, Standardbred, Thoroughbred and Arab blood has been used in the breeding of Walkers but most horses can be traced back to a Standardbred stallion, Black Allan, foaled in 1886, which is recognized as the founding sire.

PONY OF THE AMERICAS

Another relatively new breed is the Pony of the Americas. The pony resembles a miniature Appaloosa and was first produced by crossing an Appaloosa mare with a Shetland stallion. The resulting foal was a colt called Black Hand who was very successful in the show ring and as a children's pony. He became the foundation sire of the Pony of the Americas.

Leslie Boomhower of Iowa set about establishing the breed in 1956 and now these ponies can be seen in show rings all over North America. They have a conformation similar to the Shetland but with Appaloosa markings. Only ponies fulfilling these criteria may be entered in the stud book.

The ponies stand between 11.2 and 13 hands, have rounded bodies with plenty of girth and well-muscled quarters.

Below: The Pony of the Americas has a small Arab-like head with a slightly concave profile. Active and versatile, it is an easily managed children's pony.

There are over 60 recognized breeds of pony and Britain is fortunate to have nine of them as natives, ranging from the world renowned Shetland to the beautiful Welsh ponies. At the other end of the scale the biggest of the heavy horses, the Shire, has its origins in Britain yet is popular all over the world.

SHIRE

Shires, the 'gentle giants' of the horse world, are descended from the 'Great Horses of England' who used to carry men to war in Elizabethan times. In the 16th century the Great Horses had to be incredibly strong as their purpose was to carry a man in full armour or draw carts across difficult terrain.

Today's Shires are just as impressive and strong — they are the tallest and heaviest cold-blood horses and have played a vital role in England's history, particularly in the agricultural sphere.

Although mechanisation has replaced Shires as working animals in most farming areas there are still some adherents to the old traditions so the stirring sight of Shires ploughing the land can still be seen. Another popular role for these huge animals, which generally stand over 17 hands, is as dray horses for breweries. (Dray is the name given to a brewer's cart.)

Despite progress, interest in Shires remains high and there is no more magnificent sight than the Grand Parade at the Shire Horse Show when well over a hundred majestic animals are on display.

Bays, browns, blacks and greys are the usual colours for this breed and individuals often have a considerable amount of white on their legs and feet. Shires have Roman noses, large barrelled bodies and luxuriously feathered legs.

Below: *Despite their bulk, Shires can still be graceful. These gentle giants are guaranteed to draw a crowd of admirers, especially when a mare has a foal trotting beside her.*

SHETLAND PONY

They may be small but Shetlands have nonetheless made their mark on the horse world. Although one of the smallest breeds of pony they are the strongest member of the equine family in relation to their size. Shetlands are bred throughout the world and are used for general riding, driving or kept simply as a companion.

For centuries Shetland ponies have lived in the Isles from which they take their name. Situated to the north of Scotland, the islands have very severe winters and it is not unknown for the ponies to have to eat seaweed before the Spring grass comes through to provide welcome fresh grazing.

On the islands the ponies have been used as pack animals, carting peat and seaweed, as well as a means of transport.

Demand for Shetland ponies boomed in the 19th century when they were used in the coal pits of Durham in the north of Britain and other areas. As demand increased, the quality of the ponies decreased and in 1870 Lord Londonderry established a stud in Bressay and Noss to supply ponies for his mines. Over a hundred years later, almost all

Above: All the ponies which live in the New Forest are owned by people who have commoner's rights to graze animals there.

Below: Their small size and good nature make Shetlands popular and versatile mounts for children.

FACT FILE

- Shires may weigh over a ton, yet they are extremely kind and gentle.

- Shires take their name from the Shire counties of England from which they originate — Leicestershire, Derbyshire, Staffordshire and so on.

- Stone Age drawings in caves in France and Spain show ponies with Shetland features.

Shetland show ponies are descended from the Londonderry Stud.

Shetlands stand only 10.2 hands (100cm; 40in) high as an average. The Shetland was the first of Britain's native breeds to have its own breed society and registered stock must not exceed 106cm (42in) at four years old.

The foundation colour of this breed is black, although brown, grey, chestnut, bay and coloured Shetlands may be seen. In spite of their stocky appearance, Shetlands have a very light action.

NEW FOREST PONY

As long ago as the 11th century, in the time of King Canute, wild horses lived in the New Forest area of Hampshire. Now the 24,000-hectare (60,000-acre) tract is mainly grass and heather with a few wooded areas but the ponies are still there.

The New Forest Pony is Britain's second largest native pony and is probably the least wild of the British breeds. New Forests are divided into two types: ponies up to 13.2 hands, and those that are 13.2-14.2 hands and have more bone and substance. These ponies make an excellent ride for children, and the taller, stronger ones are able to carry adults as well, making the breed ideal as a family pet.

Over the centuries many other breeds have freely roamed the New Forest and at times breeds have been deliberately introduced to improve the standard of the wild ponies. In the 13th century, for example, Welsh mares lived in the Forest, and others to be introduced have included Clydesdales, Hackneys, Arabs and Thoroughbreds. In 1852, Queen Victoria allowed an Arab stallion called Zorah to roam the Forest for eight years in order to improve the stock. Since the 1930s, however, outside blood has not been allowed into the breed.

The New Forest Pony is usually brown or bay, though most other colours are accepted, and it should have long sloping shoulders, a deep body, powerful quarters and straight legs. Ponies are regularly rounded up to be branded or sold, and have been exported across the world.

49

DALES PONY

Dales ponies are bred on the eastern side of the English Pennines whilst their smaller relations, the Fells, are bred on the western side. They have a long history of working and it is only comparatively recently that they have been used as pleasure animals.

They are of Celtic descent although the influence of other breeds such as the Yorkshire Roadster is shown by the ability of Dales ponies to trot at speed. However, it was a Welsh trotting cob named Comet that had the most influence upon the current Dales ponies. He was brought to the area in the 19th century to compete in local trotting matches which were a popular pastime. Comet's ability was such that he could trot for 16km (10 miles) carrying a 76kg (170lb) man in just 33 minutes. He was put to the local mares and sired many good Dales.

For centuries Dales had been used as pack animals, transporting lead from the moors to the coast, or working on the farms as both carting and riding animals. However, the advent of heavy machinery and the car reduced their usefulness and the breed was in danger of dying out. By the mid-1950s, there were only four registered ponies.

Fortunately, the growing interest in pleasure riding led to the Dales once again being in demand, this time in pony trekking stables. With their tractable temperaments, sure-footedness, sensible and kind natures they proved themselves ideal for this work. Now Dales carry tourists over areas which once their ancestors trod.

Dales measure between 13.2 and 14.2 hands. They should have powerful bodies with muscular quarters, a neat pony-like head, good sloping shoulders, strong feet with a little feather on the heels and plenty of mane and tail hair.

CONNEMARA PONY

The small bleak area of Western Ireland known as Connemara is home to a group of tough ponies whose origins are shrouded in romance. These ponies have lived wild in Connemara for centuries but they have a touch of class not seen in other mountain ponies, being both beautiful and athletic.

Legend has it that the indigenous Irish ponies received an infusion of Spanish blood from horses which came ashore when some galleons of the Spanish Armada were wrecked in 1588. However, it is more likely that the oriental beauty evident in the Connemara results from Arab stallions imported by rich Galway merchants over three centuries ago. Some of these escaped and joined the wild herds.

Some experts think that the Connemara is based on the same stock as the Highland, Shetland, Icelandic and Norwegian Fjord ponies. It is certainly more athletic than an ordinary mountain pony. When cross-bred with a horse, it tends to produce sizeable competition horses. When Connemaras are kept in a better environment, warm and well fed, they usually grow larger than when left on their bleak native homeland territory.

FACT FILE

• Connemaras were used in their native Ireland as working ponies, carting peat and turf.

• The original colour of Connemaras was a yellowish dun, although grey is the colour most often seen now.

• With their placid temperament and sure-footedness, Dales are used for shepherding in northern Britain.

Below: *Dales are usually black but bays and browns are also found. These ponies should not exceed 14.2 hands.*

The toughness of the Connemaras derives from the conditions under which the ponies have lived. Their natural habitat is bogs and mountains, with sparse grazing. In addition, they often endure severe weather conditions owing to Atlantic gales.

Although the local people have always used Connemaras as pack and riding animals it was not until the start of the 20th century that outside interest was expressed. The Irish Government decided to preserve and improve the breed and in 1928 a breed society was formed. Now the Connemara pony, which reaches a height of 13-14.2 hands, is a more uniform type than would have been seen at the start of this century. It has also become firmly established in the USA, Australia and Europe.

DARTMOOR PONY

For centuries ponies have roamed over the large tracts of moorland in Devon in South West England known as Dartmoor. These rock-strewn moors are over 300m (1000ft) above sea level and the native ponies to which they are home have proved to be tough but quality animals.

There is a reference to the Dartmoor pony as early as 1012, in the will of a Saxon bishop named Aelfwold of Crediton. But it was not until the 19th century that interest was shown in defining the breed.

Dartmoor ponies were once used to transport tin from the mines to the town and

Above: The athletic Connemaras have a widespread reputation for versatility and usefulness in competition. They are also hardy, able to withstand severe weather.

Below: Dartmoor ponies have been exported and breeding goes on in countries other than Britain. But they are still bred on Dartmoor itself, in South West England.

to carry farmers to market. Now they are very popular as children's riding ponies. The Dartmoor is also useful as foundation stock for breeding larger riding animals.

Dartmoors are comfortable rides due to their free low action and their good front — the shoulders are set back so that riders feel as if there is more in front of them. Apart from their versatility and equable temperaments, they are also economic to keep, which has added to their popularity.

When small ponies were in great demand for use in mines, a number of Shetlands were allowed to run free on the moor in order to mate with the native ponies. However, this resulted in a degeneration of the Dartmoor stock, so after the Second World War attempts were made to improve standards. Only ponies passed by inspection or being placed at specific shows were allowed to be included in the Stud Book.

Most of today's Dartmoors can be traced back to a stallion named The Leat who was allowed to act as a stud in 1920. The Leat looked like a Dartmoor pony but was sired by a desert-born Arab. He proved to be a very successful stallion. In the 1960s there was an upsurge of interest in the Dartmoor and many of the ponies were exported.

Dartmoor ponies do not exceed 12.2 hands and are usually bay, black, brown or grey in colour. Piebalds and skewbalds are not allowed.

WELSH PONY AND COB

The ponies of Wales are some of Britain's oldest and most popular residents. Because they are so varied, they have been divided into four types (or sections) in the Stud Book.

The Welsh Mountain Pony comprises Section A and is the oldest and smallest of the four types, thought to have lived in the hills for over a 1000 years. Many people feel it is the most beautiful of the British breeds, and its pretty head reflects the influence of the Arab (probably introduced in Roman times). It reaches 12.2 hands and is in great demand as a child's riding pony.

The Welsh Pony Section B is known as the riding pony of this group, although it does not exceed 13.2 hands. The Welsh Pony Section C is a stockier pony of Cob type which also reaches 13.2 hands. It is believed to be the result of Mountain ponies crossed with Andalusians.

Section D is the Welsh Cob, which stands 14.2-15.2 hands in height. Welsh Cobs have carried armies as well as being used for general farm work and shepherding. They have also influenced other breeds such as Morgans and Hackneys. Very impressive in trot, Welsh Cobs have a high-stepping action.

EXMOOR PONY

Exmoor ponies take their name from the moor in South West England over which they roam. They are the only Mountain and Moorland breed to have existed in Britain

FACT FILE

- Oriental blood was first introduced into the Welsh Mountain Pony bloodline by Julius Caesar, who founded a stud of these ponies.

- Every year in autumn, the Exmoor ponies living on the moor are rounded up for inspection and branding.

- Highland ponies are one of the oldest breeds, but their origins are obscure. Throughout their history, they have had infusions of Arab blood.

Below: Welsh ponies are known for their hardiness, soundness and versatility. Infusions of Arab and Thoroughbred blood have helped to improve the breed.

from earliest times, descended from the wild ponies which the Ancient Britons rode.

The ponies are characterized by the mealy colour found on their muzzles, around the eyes, on the underbelly and inside of their flanks. Another feature is their 'toad' eyes which are prominent, large and wide set.

Exmoor ponies have to survive severe winter conditions on the moor which is reflected in the special texture of their thick, harsh coats. Bay, brown and dun are the major colours with no white markings. Stallions reach a height of 12.3 hands while the standard for mares is 12.2 hands. Despite their small stature, Exmoors are very strong and will carry full-grown men across the moor, either for farm work or hunting.

Right: Exmoors are extremely tough ponies with tremendous powers of endurance. They are also adept at looking after their riders.

Below: Highlands have compact, powerful bodies with strong quarters, good shoulders, pronounced withers and strong arched necks.

HIGHLAND PONY

The Scottish Highlands and the Western Isles are home to the largest and strongest of Britain's native breeds — the Highland Pony. This is a very old breed, and its members are believed to be descendants of ponies from Northern Asia who moved west across Europe after the Ice Age.

Highland ponies fall into two types, the Western Isle ponies which are smaller, standing 12.2-13.2 hands, and the Mainland ponies who reach 14.2 hands. The strength of these animals is well known: they have been used to carry deer for stalkers — and stags can weigh as much as 130kg (280lb)!

Sure-footed and well balanced with naturally good paces, particularly at walk and trot, Highland ponies are extremely versatile. They have been a major form of transport in their home area throughout history, both under saddle and in harness. Today, whilst they are still used for farm work, these strong, docile ponies are also popular as general riding animals, for showing, driving and as foundation stock. Of necessity, these ponies are hardy animals, possessing a winter coat with a difference: a soft dense undercoat, covered by thick, coarse hair. Dun, grey, black and brown are accepted colours for Highlands and many have an eel stripe along their back. Zebra markings on the legs are also seen.

53

Below: Pure-bred Austrian Haflingers can be recognized by the mark with which they are all branded — the shape of an edelweiss (Austria's national flower) with an 'H' in the centre. Despite their heavy build, Haflingers have a natural athleticism and balance.

Europe's breeds include horses with ancient lineage, such as the Norwegian Fjord, and relatively new breeds created for specific purposes, such as the Danish Warmblood. Some breeds have enjoyed a heyday stretching over decades, have fallen from favour and are now experiencing a revival. In their own way, they all have fascinating histories.

HAFLINGER

One of the most distinctive breeds of horses is the Haflinger which originates from Austria. Its eye-catching golden coat and lovable temperament make this hardy mountain pony popular and versatile.

The Haflinger's coat can vary from a pale palomino to a reddish chestnut. All these ponies look remarkably like their parents. The Haflinger's distinctive looks can be traced back to a part-Arab stallion who looked just like the ponies we know today. His looks have become a requisite standard for the breed.

The influence of Arab blood is reflected in the slightly dished head of the Haflingers. Friendly, intelligent and gentle, these ponies are now bred in England, America and Australia as well as Europe.

Haflingers measure 13-14.2 hands and are used for all kinds of riding activities including driving.

LIPIZZANER

Intelligent, athletic and strong, Lipizzaners are perhaps best known as the famous 'white horses' of the Spanish Riding School of Vienna. With their superb displays of 'haute ecole' or 'high school' work they have thrilled generations of horse lovers.

This is the oldest pure-bred horse in Europe and the Lipizzaner stud books have complete details going as far back as 1735, when the Viennese School was founded.

In 1580, Archduke Charles II of Austria founded a stud at Lipizza to provide the finest horses for high school work in the Austrian Court. Spanish stallions, particularly Andalusians, and Italian mares were used, although from 1700 other blood was introduced, such as German and Danish.

The present stock can be traced back to six studs, largely of Spanish descent, introduced into the breeding programme in the late 18th and early 19th century.

War brought disruption to the Lipizzaners during the Great War of 1914-1918 when Lipizza became Italian. The Austrian Lipizzaners were moved to Piber in southern Austria. Despite further disruptions during World War II, when the stud was requisitioned by the German Army, Lipizzaners con-

Above: For competition show jumping and all-round riding pleasure, the Irish Draught is a popular choice.

Below: The highest standards of classical horsemanship are maintained by the Spanish Riding School and its Lipizzaners.

tinued to be bred in Piber, Austria's only state owned stud. The horses are also still bred in Lipizza which is now part of Yugoslavia.

Lipizzaners measure 15-16 hands and are mostly grey, although bay is seen. As well as their high school work, they are also popular as harness horses in combined driving and are a natural choice for dressage.

IRISH DRAUGHT

Renowned for their versatility, Irish Draughts are a popular choice for crossing with Thoroughbreds to produce superb hunters and good competition horses, particularly for show jumping.

Throughout their history these horses have been true 'all rounders', having been used on farms for general work, ridden to hounds and then put in harness.

Nowadays, they are no longer required for farm work but are represented in many equestrian sports and are used as breeding stock. Measuring up to 17 hands, their kind natures, intelligence, strength, speed and sure-footedness add to their appeal.

Irish Draughts have been in existence since the end of the 18th century and it is likely that they are descended from horses bred in the Connemara region of Ireland. Their ability to be 'good doers' — horses which are economical to feed — led in the past to many Irish Draughts going into service with the Army.

NORWEGIAN FJORD PONY

In appearance the Norwegian Fjord pony is very like the primeval horse, with the typical dun colour (light creamy-yellow), zebra markings and dorsal stripe. These ponies have inhabited Norway since prehistoric times and the pony we see today has changed little from the times when the Vikings rode the Norwegian Fjord's ancestors to war and first introduced the ponies to ploughing.

The Norwegian Fjord originates from Western Norway and there has been very little cross breeding over the centuries. The ponies breed very true to type from generation to generation, one distinguishing feature being their upright silver mane which has a line of black hair running down the centre. The ponies usually have their manes clipped into a crescent shape to ensure that the black mane hair can be seen.

Apart from carrying men to war, these ponies have been invaluable for farm work, especially in the mountainous areas where it is difficult to use machinery.

Standing 13-14.2 hands, the Norwegian Fjord ponies are muscular and strong but with very good temperaments. They are becoming increasingly popular for both riding and driving. The breed has spread throughout Scandinavia and is especially popular in Denmark where, in the Jutland area, ponies were imported at the beginning of this century for light agricultural work. They are also seen in West Germany and Britain.

ANDALUSIAN

The Andalusian is one of the oldest breeds of horse and, until the 18th century, it was the foremost horse in Europe, seen in numerous royal courts, with a reputation for high school work. However, the turmoil on the continent, heralded by the French Revolution, saw a change of fortune for Andalusians and they diminished in popularity. Now these athletic horses are enjoying a revival of interest and are proving themselves in many equestrian disciplines.

The breed originates from Andalusia in Southern Spain and although its exact bloodlines are not known, the Spanish horse was considered to be the best in the world at the time of the Greek and Roman Empires.

Below: *The distinctive manes of the Fjord ponies are soft when the foals are born but become stiffer as the ponies grow older. These ponies are docile and long-lived.*

As Spain made its mark in other countries so the Andalusians influenced other breeds, such as the Morgan in North America and the Lipizzaner, also famous for its classical work.

The success of the Andalusian as a breed owes much to the Carthusian monks who established a stud at Jerez and bred selectively for centuries. In other areas Andalusians were crossed with other breeds to make them heavier but the monks kept the purity of the breed, never selling any mares from the stud but supplying fine stallions to many European noblemen.

Andalusians are renowned for their agility and spectacular paces. Grey is the usual colour, although bays and blacks are also seen. They stand 15-16 hands and have short, strong bodies with deep girths, long sloping shoulders, well defined withers, broad muscular hindquarters and low set tail. The mane and tail are long and luxuriant.

BRABANT

Centuries of selective breeding have produced the powerful horses known as Brabants or Belgian Heavy Draught Horses. They are heavy horses with small heads in comparison to their hefty bodies. They have short backs, deep girths, and short, feathered legs. Brabants are calm and docile.

Brabants are direct descendants of the Flanders horses, renowned in medieval times as the mounts of knights in their heavy armour. Although very little outside blood has been introduced into their lines, these horses have influenced other European heavy horse breeds such as the Ardennes.

During World War I many European horse breeds suffered, including around 20,000 Brabants which were requisitioned by the German Army for military service. This number represented about a fifth of the entire breed population.

Standing between 15.3 and 16.3 hands high, the Brabant is usually red roan or chestnut in colour. The strength, work capacity and temperament of the Brabant have made it a popular choice as a work horse in its homeland and abroad. Many have been exported to the United States. In addition to their traditional role, Brabants are now driven for pleasure.

Left: *Andalusians have an ancient and noble ancestry. They were often ridden by European monarchs, and at one time the export of breeding stock from Spain was forbidden.*

Below: *About 700 Brabant foals are registered annually in Belgium. In the USA and Canada Brabants have been bred to produce lighter coats.*

CAMARGUE

The Camargue area of France is famous for its 'white horses' and black bulls, and romantic tales about the region capture the imagination of many people.

The wild horses are an ancient breed with obscure origins, although the Camargue is thought to be descended from prehistoric breeds crossed with oriental blood such as Arabs and Barbs. Home for them is the swampy delta of the Rhone in southern France where they roam in small herds. Usually the herds consist of one stallion with mares of different ages and colts up to three years. Regular round-ups ensure that foals are branded and some colts are gelded so that the breed standard can be controlled.

Below: Camargues are usually between 13.1 to 14.1 hands. They roam wild in small herds which consist of one stallion, colts up to three years old and mares.

Since becoming an officially recognized breed in 1968 more selective breeding policies have been introduced with only the better stallions and mares being allowed to run free and breed.

Although essentially wild creatures, a number of Camargues are caught and broken for riding — once trained, they prove to be agile, sure-footed rides. Because they are active and able to twist and turn quickly they are used by the local 'gardiens' or cowboys to herd the famous black bulls of the Camargue, for round-ups and for escorting the bulls to the bull rings. Trained Camargues are also used as trekking ponies for the tourist trade and as pack animals.

Surviving on the rough grass of the salt marsh and swampland, the Camargues are

FACT FILE

• Camargue foals are born black but become white as they mature.

• Although slow to mature, Camargues live to a great age.

• In Germany, the Westphalian is the second most numerous regional breed. First place is held by the Hanoverian.

Left: *Fire, a Westphalian who captured the world showjumping crown. Westphalians came to prominence in showjumping in 1978 when Roman became World Champion.*

has come from the neighbouring German warm-blood, the Hanoverian. Originally more of a farm and army horse, the Westphalian's development into a leading competition breed, has been made possible by the introduction of Hanoverian blood.

The success of the breed continues thanks to a rigorous selection policy at the state stud of Warendorf. Stallions are tested for riding and jumping ability, their temperaments are carefully observed, and their willingness to work, character and constitution are also carefully monitored. Only the best stallions are allowed to stand at stud.

Westphalians stand 15.2-16.2 hands in height and are heavier and more substantial than Hanoverians. They are found in all solid colours and have intelligent heads, well-proportioned, muscular bodies and strong quarters.

DANISH WARMBLOOD

This is a recently created breed of sporting horse which is now in considerable demand as it is a versatile competition horse. Famous Danish Warmbloods include the three day event horse Monaco, whose honours include the European Championship, and Marzog, the dressage silver medallist at the 1984 Olympic Games.

The breed came about because Denmark, once a foremost country in horse breeding, was, in the post war years, having to import horses for its serious competition riders. In the 1960s it was decided to lay the foundations for a national breed although the societies and breeders concerned did not receive any government assistance.

The breed was developed using German, British and Swedish stock. Selective and strict breeding meant that two decades later Denmark was providing its own home-grown champions and exporting its horses to other countries.

Danish Warmbloods stand 15.3-17 hands and may be any colour, although bay is the most common. As it is a relatively new warm-blood, the stud book has a number of types registered. Danish Warmbloods are known for their athleticism and even temperaments. These qualities, combined with their generous natures, have enabled this breed to excel in the dressage arena.

Right: *Danish Warmbloods are proof of how selective breeding can produce top class horses to fulfil specific demands, such as champions in the dressage arena.*

tough and hardy horses, although they are not the most elegant, having rather large heads and straight shoulders. But Camargues are robust and are famous for their powers of endurance. Measuring 13.1-14.1 hands, they have strong short backs, deep girths, good legs with plenty of bone (indicating an ability to carry weight) and hard feet. Unusually, their ears are placed more to the side than other breeds. Although slow to mature, they live to a great age.

WESTPHALIAN

Westphalians originate in Germany but are known throughout the world because they excel in competition. Show jumping, dressage, eventing and driving are four equestrian disciplines in which Westphalians have made their mark. Perhaps the most famous example of this breed is the renowned dressage horse Ahlerich, ridden by Reiner Klimke to World Championship and Olympic honours.

The Westphalian is not pure-bred. Thoroughbreds have been used to improve the breed but perhaps the biggest influence

OTHER POPULAR BREEDS

Below: Visitors to Iceland can see this beautiful country from the back of an Icelandic pony. With their unusual gaits, they make comfortable rides as well as friendly companions.

There is a great variety of horses and ponies existing in many different countries, developed according to each country's own particular needs. For example, the Bashkir pony of the USSR is a means of transport, food, milk, clothing and shelter for the tribes people, whilst in Denmark a new competition horse has been selectively bred. What follows is a small selection of other popular breeds from various countries of the world, although once again the influence of truly international breeds such as the Thoroughbred and Arab can be seen.

ICELANDIC PONY

The native ponies of Iceland differ from other ponies in that they have two extra gaits, the tolt and the pace, in addition to the normal walk, trot and canter. The tolt is a four-time action which is also known as run-

ning walk or rack. It is a very rhythmic movement and gives a smoother ride than the trot.

The pace is a two-time action which gives the rider the impression that the pony is floating. This is because both legs on the same side move together and there is a moment of suspension when all four hooves are off the ground.

The first ponies were taken to Iceland when it was settled in AD 871 by Norwegians. Other settlers from Norse colonies in Scotland and Ireland also introduced ponies which interbred to produce the Icelandic pony.

There are special competitions for Icelandics because of their unusual gaits. However, they are also used for many other equestrian activities as well as farm work. Although the average height is only 13 hands, these hardy ponies are strong enough to carry adults. All colours and markings are seen.

AUSTRALIAN STOCK HORSE

A more robust version of the Thoroughbred, the Australian Stock Horse is known for its agility, courage, stamina, hardiness and turn of speed.

Horses were not found in Australia until they were introduced by settlers in the 18th century. Cross breeding of Arabs, Thoroughbreds and Anglo-Arabs with mares of various blood resulted in the Australian Waler, named after the New South Wales region of Australia where the breeding was concentrated. These were cavalry horses also used for herding cattle and in harness. With the introduction of more Arab and Thoroughbred blood this century, the Waler became known as the Australian Stock Horse.

Stock Horses may be any colour and vary in height from 14.2-16 hands. With their versatility they have scored successes in en-

FACT FILE

- Icelandics have remained pure-bred for over 1000 years.

- The Russians led the world in harness racing with the Orlov Trotter, from which was bred the Russian Trotter.

- Perhaps the most famous Australian Stock Horse in competition was Regal Realm, the event horse. Partnered by Britain's Lucinda Green, he won the World Event Championship.

durance riding, polo, jumping and racing as well as being in demand for working cattle and sheep stations. They are also the most popular campdrafting horses in Australia. This fast sport involves the horses turning on a coin, galloping from a standstill and halting within a stride, as well as separating a bullock from a group and driving it around a set course in a set time.

A breed society has been in existence since the 1970s to control and promote the breed.

Above: *Stock Horses have achieved success in international competition as well as being invaluable for working cattle and sheep.*

Below: *American and Russian blood combined to produce the Russian Trotter — a fast breed for harness racing. The horse is the result of American Standardbreds crossed with Orlov Trotters.*

RUSSIAN TROTTER

Also known as the Metis Trotter, the Russian Trotter is a light but robust horse with a tough, muscular build. It was derived from another Russian breed, the Orlov Trotter — the supreme harness racing horse of the early days of the sport. Towards the end of the 19th century, however, the Orlov Trotter was surpassed by the American Standardbred. Taking the best of both worlds, breeders crossed the Orlov Trotter with imported American horses to produce a faster horse — the Russian Trotter. The breed was officially recognized in 1949.

These horses have a flowing action but their hind feet tend to move outwards in a semicircular movement. When the horse lengthens his stride this peculiarity of action helps him to establish a long reaching pace more easily.

Russian Trotters stand 15-15.3 hands in height and the usual colour is bay, although black, grey and chestnut are also seen. Energetic movers, they nonetheless have docile temperaments.

CASPIAN PONY

Caspians are unlike any other ponies — in appearance they resemble a well bred horse, but in miniature.

This ancient breed was thought to be extinct but in 1965 a tiny stallion was seen pulling a heavy cart around a northern Iranian town. He was bought by Louise Firouz who immediately started searching for more like him. Other diminutive horses were found on the shores of the Caspian Sea and in the surrounding mountains.

The ponies are thought to be descendants of the miniature horse of Mesopotamia, an ancient civilization that existed in the Middle East 5000 years ago. These ancient horses were probably the forerunners of many breeds including the Arab.

When the Caspians were saved from extinction it is thought that only about 50 of them were in existence. They had been bred only in a small area of Iran but this had the advantage of preserving the ancient breed, without any infusions of other blood.

Political upheaval in their native country meant that some Caspians had to be exported to ensure the survival of the breed. Caspians are now bred in Britain, New Zealand, America, Canada and Australia.

The Caspian reaches 10-12 hands and its fine appearance belies its strength. For centuries it has been used as a work horse but now it is popular for driving and as a children's pony.

BASHKIR PONY

The thickset Bashkir ponies originate from the Urals in the USSR where they have been used for centuries by the Bashkiri people as work animals, for transport and for food.

Measuring up to 13.3 hands, the ponies are unusual in that the younger mares will produce as much as 14-28 litres (3-6 gals) of milk per day. The Bashkiri people keep the mares in milking herds and use the milk both as a drink and for making cream and butter. They also make it into an alcoholic drink which they claim has medicinal properties. The ponies are also used for meat and clothing.

To survive the freezing temperatures of their homelands the Bashkir ponies have thick, curly winter coats. The hair may be

FACT FILE

• Native-bred Caspian ponies are between 10 and 12 hands; those bred elsewhere tend to be bigger.

• Bashkir ponies can survive temperatures as low as −40°C (−40°F).

• Falabellas have two fewer ribs and two fewer vertebrae than other horses.

Left: *Caspians have fine Arab-type heads and wide set eyes. Colours may be bay, chestnut, brown or grey. They jump well and make ideal mounts for children.*

There are several stories about the origins of these finely built horses — one relates the tale of horses trapped in a deep canyon with poor food supplies. Over the generations the horses became smaller until they were found and rescued by the Falabella family.

However, the true origins of these tiny horses is reputed to lie with one tiny stallion who was found in the 19th century. The Indians described the stallion as having 'dwarf sickness'. No-one actually knows where the stallion was from or who originally owned him, yet it was the offspring of this stallion that was to form the basis of the entire Falabella breed.

It was found that crossing the stallion with larger breeds resulted in offspring that were much smaller than their mothers. Over several generations the size of the original miniature horse was achieved. Falabellas have now been bred for 130 years and, as they have been crossed with many breeds,

all kinds of colours and markings are found. Spotted ones, however, are less common.

Stallions cannot mate directly with the larger mares and so fertilization is achieved by artificial insemination. The foals are usually about 40-55cm (16-21in) high at birth. Unlike other horses, which continue to grow until they are six years old, Falabellas achieve most of their height in their first year. By the time they are three Falabellas are fully grown.

In terms of care, Falabellas need similar treatment to fine ponies and Thoroughbreds, except in smaller quantities. However, they are not strong enough to be ridden and are kept only as pets and companions. They are easily trained, have kind temperaments and enjoy human company.

As well as being bred on the Falabella ranch in Argentina, these tiny horses are also bred in Britain at the Kilverstone Stud in Norfolk. They have been exposed all over the world, and still breed true.

Left: *Bashkir ponies are strong and sensible, ideal as pack animals in rough country. In their homelands, their duties include pulling sleighs through the snow.*

Below: *The diminutive Falabella is the smallest horse breed. The horses are kept as pets since they are too small to be ridden and also need a certain amount of pampering.*

up to 15cm (6in) long, and the mane and tail are extremely thick. Bay, chestnut and light brown are the most common colours.

It is thought that some Bashkir ponies were taken to Alaska by the Russians, because at the end of the 19th century a breed was discovered in Nevada, USA, which closely resembled the Bashkir. These American ponies also have curly coats, with fine manes and tails.

FALABELLA

This rare breed of horse was developed and named by the Falabella family in Argentina. Although Falabellas stand under 8.2 hands (less than 86cm; 34in) they are miniature horses, not ponies. They have perfect proportions so that gazing upon a Falabella is like looking at a scaled down model of a horse — a perfect horse in miniature.

INDEX